T0066797

The Startup Habit

The Startup Habit

The Right Habits to Fuel
The Entrepreneur in You

Dr. K C C Nair; Dr. Arun Surendran

PARTRIDGE

ISBN: Softcover   978-1-4828-7380-1
              eBook   978-1-4828-7379-5

To order additional copies of this book, contact
Partridge India
000 800 10062 62
orders.india@partridgepublishing.com

www.partridgepublishing.com/india

Contents

The Startup Habit

Dr. KCC Nair
Founder, Technopark Technology
Business Incubator & Founder Member,
Technopark, Trivandrum

Dr. Arun Surendran
Strategic Director, Trinity College of
Engineering

With Foreword By
Shri. Kochouseph Chittillappilly

Foreword

We live in an era when a lot of predictions are made of which country will claim top slots in the global economy in the coming decades. I believe we are poised to claim the rightful slot if the young-India say YES to an entrepreneurship culture. Dr. K. C. Chandrasekharan Nair & Dr. Arun Surendran's this book *The Startup Habit*, born out of a perfect amalgam of knowledge and experience, will certainly be a beacon to show the way forward for those who fondle entrepreneurial dreams.

When we were kids growing up, we were taught that 'Knowledge is Power'. But as we live through the varied facets of life we realize that without experience there will never be true knowledge. We might think we know, but only with experience will we have anything more than grasping an idea. However, they are not two separate entities; rather comparing knowledge and experience is like comparing nuts and bolts – when entwined together, they perform the best.

To transform the seeds of lingering ideas into successful full-blown ventures we need both knowledge and experience. We come across a good number of hardworking people around us. But many of them fail to achieve success in life, because to be successful, hard work should blend harmoniously with ideas, knowledge and experience to survive in this fast-changing, competitive world. For those who contemplate an entrepreneurial career, ideas and knowledge are readily available, but lack of experience is the risk factor that bothers them.

Here is where *The Startup Habit* comes to play. The wealth of unmatched experience shared by KCC, the 'father of business incubation in Kerala' himself, who have nurtured over 200 start-up companies from the incubator, and the in-depth knowledge of Dr. Arun Surendran, who is a veteran of creating vibrant start-up culture within campuses, will prove to be a treasure trove and constant companion in your entrepreneurial journey. Let me reiterate, the accounts of practical management wisdom narrated by the authors will never fail to quicken those entertaining an entrepreneurial dream; inspire those already into business and are at a dilemma as to how to take it to the next level; or even might awaken the dormant seeds of entrepreneurship in those of you who've never thought of entering into business.

In short, I wish I were to find such a priceless wealth of knowledge and experience on business treasured in a book when I began my entrepreneurial journey. Little did I know, then, the must-have qualities, attitudes, habits and approaches every wannabe-successful-entrepreneur should have. I am happy that *The Startup Habit* is in your hands, and I hope every word and example in this book ease your own journey toward success!

- Kochouseph Chittilappilly

Acknowledgement

In 2004 October, Department of Science & Technology (DST), Government of India and InfoDev, World Bank together organised the first Global Forum on Business Incubation in New Delhi. Mr V J Jayakumar, The then CEO of Technopark got an invitation to attend the conference. But due to certain personal problems, he was not able to go for the conference. He informed his inability to the other senior team members and sought their interest to participate; no one was interested to attend. Then he came to me and asked me whether I was interested. I agreed and went to Delhi to attend the conference and that's where I started my Incubation Journey. I remember the Keltronians in Technopark Team who inspired and supported me throughout my journey, GVR, KGS, KR, MV, VJJ and finally RK Nair who every now and then reminded me to "quit the CFO position and take up

Incubation and Entrepreneurship development activities with Technopark Technology Business Incubator" as full time Director. He was the then CEO of Technopark.

In December 2005 I got a chance to hear a motivational speech of the then president of India Dr APJ Abdul Kalam which had an electrifying effect and it literally transformed me to be a mentor for startups. I accepted the challenge then and there. And I got a second chance to meet him in Delhi in 2008 May during the National Technology Day celebrations organised by DST, Government of India when me and Sri RK Nair received the Best Technology Incubator in India award for 2007 from him and got his blessings!

The other two personalities influenced me most are Sri Harkesh Kumar Mittal, Head of NSTEDB, DST, and Dr A S Rao who was the Advisor to Department of scientific & Industrial Research (DSIR), Government of India. They supported me throughout my career with TTBI to make my Incubator the world's 2nd Best! Sri H K Mittal planned for the National Advisory Committee Meeting in 2006 at Technopark Trivandrum and gave us the approval for the Technopark Technology Business Incubator (TTBI), and this was one of the 1st TBIs approved outside the campus of an educational Institution in India. The huge success of this Incubator motivated him to approve our next proposal to start the Startup Village (ITIH TBI) in Kochi after 6 years as a PPP model.

I remember my friends and colleagues in DST and DSIR in Delhi Dr Anita Gupta, Sri Praveen Roy, Sri Pratap

Singh, Dr Sujith Banerji to name a few; thank you all friends.

I remember my friends and motivators from InfoDev, World Bank, Sri Vivek Chaudhary (World Bank), Julian Webb (Australia), Mercedes Barcelon (Manila), Richard White (New Zealand), Seth Ayers (World Bank), Peter Harman (UKBI). When the WB Team came for the second ISBA Conference in Technopark Trivandrum in 2008, they always requested for arranging logistics, local transportation etc, and all the time I made it possible by telling no problem friend. Vivek Chaudhary then onwards called me by a nick name "Mr No Problem Nair". I am fondly accepting the name Vivek, thank you very much for Recognising my commitment to Incubation. Their help and support made me to attend the 2nd Global Forum in Nov 2006 at Hyderabad, 3rd in Oct 2009 at Florianopolis, Brazil and the 4th in Helsinki, Finland.

It will be a thankless job from my side if I don't remember Sri KPP Nambiar who gave me the chance to be a member of the Founding Team of Technopark, Sri Rajendra kumar M K, the then Registrar of ER& DC and Dr Rao C Kasarabada who referred me to KPP.

I remember my Indian Incubator friends Dr Biju Jacob, NH Incubator Bangaluru, Sri RMP Jawahar, Trichi, Dr Raghunandan, Delhi, Dr PKB Menon, Delhi, Sri Balachandran, VITTBI, Dr Sureshkumar APIN, Karuppanchetty, ICRIST, Hyderabad, Sri Rahul

Patwardhan, CEO, IndiaCo ventures and the entire ISBA Team for the support and hand holding.

I acknowledge my thanks to my Incubator team, especially Mr Sreejith for untainted support to me to make my dream a reality. My dream now is to transform Kerala into a Startup State by 2020. I *Also remember with sincere thanks* my Finance team at Technopark, without their support I could not spent extra time working with the Incubator.

I remember my first Startup team, the Torque (MobMe) who graduated from TTBI and founded the Startup Village with me; thanks Sanjay and Team. I acknowledge the support of Arun Balachandran, CEO of NRI TBI, Kochi, Hrishikesh Nair, CEO of Infopark and CEO of TTBI after me, Deepak Raveedran, CEO Innoz, The CEOs of Technopark companies, VK Mathews, K Nandakumar, Mr Ansar Shahabudeen, the team TBIG, Smt Aruna Sunderarajan, IAS, Additional Chief Secretary to Government of Kerala, Sri K M Chandrasekhar, Vice Chairman, Kerala State Planning Board, Sri Cyriac Davis MD of KITCO and his team. I sincerely acknowledge the support and encouragement extended to me by Sri. P K Kunhalikutty, Minister for IT, Industries and Social Welfare, Government of Kerala. Finally I thank all the media persons who supported me throughout my 36 years careers specially Sri Mathukutty, J Kunnappally and Sri sajeev kumar C N.

My friend Mr Sanil Kumar who is with the Trinity College of Engineering working as their GM administration called me one day and requested me to visit their college in Trivandrum to speak to their students on Entrepreneurship. I met Dr Arun Surendran, the Strategic Director of the College during the function. Later we discussed on student entrepreneurship scenario in Kerala. We came to understand that our thought process is same on this. Later we spent evenings in different hangouts in the city and finally motivated each other start working on a project like this. We spent Sundays at Zenzerro Restaurant in the city, discussed, drafted and redrafted and finally "The Startup Habit" was born. I thank my co-author Dr Arun Surendran to take up the initiative to make this happen.

Last but not the least, immense gratitude to the visionary and veteran entrepreneur of Kerala, Shri Kochouseph Chittilappilly who was kind and encouraging to provide a wonderfully inspiring foreword for the book.

Thank Almighty God to enable me thrive through all the bad times, fight with all the odds to reach to the shore of success in my life with promoting Innovation, Incubation and entrepreneurship activities and motivating the Student Entrepreneurs in the State of Kerala and enable them to take up Entrepreneurship as a career and a Habit.

Dr. KCC Nair

I would like to thank Dr. Thomas Alexander, the Chief Executive Director of Al Adrak and the Chairman of Trinity College of Engineering for being the greatest mentor any entrepreneur could have hoped for. His incredible vision, clarity of articulation and down to earth approach continues to inspire us at Trinity College to forge ahead with our dreams. Special thanks to the warm and vibrant Trinity College family which has the unique reputation of a campus with entrepreneur-professors. Jimmy Bentex, Vivek Stanley, Jayakrishnan and Deepu Sajeev are few of the faculty entrepreneurs who have helped immensely with the idea and the content of the book.

We are grateful for everyone who supported by sharing generously with us their experiences, good and bad, in their startup journeys. Special thanks to entrepreneur-actor-chef Anand whose Zenzerro Café in Trivandrum served as the meeting place for crucial discussions and drafting of the book. My heartfelt gratitude to Dr. KCC Nair, for his limitless energy and dedication for the Startup movement in this nation, for this book and for finding out the teacher and entrepreneur in me.

As always I remain grateful to my family for being the strength and support for all my endeavors.

Dr. Arun Surendran

Dedication

I dedicate this book to my wife Smt K N Omana for her wonderful support and togetherness throughout my career for all these years. I left her alone in home for many days with children when I was on travel, but she managed the home, managed the children, managed me and her job altogether. I dedicate the book to my children and to the entire Startup Community and the Student Entrepreneurs in Kerala with a request to make Kerala the Best startup location in the world.

Dr. KCC Nair

Dedicated

to my inspiring parents, Surendran Nair and Chandrika Devi, who effortlessly play the roles of friends and mentors in my life and to my extended loving family at the Trinity College of Engineering.

Dr. Arun Surendran

Why The Startup Habit?

Why the habit and why the book? :-)

The year was 2006. A sweaty humid June afternoon on a fan-less dais of a cavernous college auditorium in Kerala!

Dr. K.C. Chandrasekharan Nair shifted uncomfortably on his claustrophobically armed wooden chair behind a ceremonially frilled table with the quintessential flower vase. He forced a smile as the aged professor at the podium finished his nearly half hour long tirade with the following admonition, waving a menacing finger towards Dr. KCC Nair : "Do not listen to this man. He is asking you to take risks. Your future will be uncertain.

You are better off studying hard for your exams, and then look for a safe, secure, salaried job!"

It was the inauguration of the Innovation and Entrepreneurship Development Center (IEDC) in one of Kerala's leading engineering colleges; one of the the first IEDCs in the state of Kerala. The audience were final year engineering students and their faculty. The accuser who finished with the flourishing warning was the Principal of the college; a veteran with over 35 years of teaching experience in engineering.

This was the beginning of KCC's campaign to spur the entrepreneurial bug in the engineering college campuses of Kerala. It was an ominous start.

Much has changed since those days of verbally violent resistance against change among the faculty and experienced educators.

As the Managing Director of the Technology Business Incubator at the Technopark in Trivandrum, Dr Nair, lovingly known as KCC, nurtured over 200 companies into existence. Their total revenue today is well over Rupees 250 crores. The road was never easy. Yet slowly but surely, the momentum has built.

Cafes and bakeries are excellent spots to get a good grasp, albeit unscientific, of the latest thought trends amidst the Indian youth. Couple of years ago, any such snack bar in Thiruvananthapuram would have given the impression that all youngsters are waiting to break into movies. Today, innovation and entrepreneurship provide the heady mix along with the wafting aromas of coffee and baked goodies even in a laid back small city like Thiruvananthapuram.

India's youth, from Coimbatore to Kota and Surat to Shillong, are starting up!

The nation cannot employee its massive young workforce through the government, public sector units or a few large companies.

Entrepreneurship is a necessity! It is a necessity now!

As the youngest nation in the world is rapidly claiming its place of glory on the planet, plenty remains to be done. For several years now, both the proponents and opponents of entrepreneurship have been asking the same question, "Why hasn't India produced a Google? Or a Facebook? Or a Samsung? Or a Hyundai?"

The search for quick, simple causes leads to the usual culprits of poverty, population, corruption. Some even consider the Indian mindset, as if such a universal mindset really exists, to be genetically wired against starting up and chronically geared towards safe job seeking.

A cursory look at the statistics, however, reveals a totally different picture. Several thousand companies are registered each year in India. By 2014, in Kerala alone after the government announced a plan to support

1000 start up companies in 10 years, 800 companies were registered in under two years. Prime Minister Shri Narendra Modi has unveiled a far more ambitious and ground breaking Start Up India campaign in early 2016.

Even so, the statistically straightforward answer to the delay in an Indian Google's arrival can be seen as we compare the start up rates of the United States, Israel and South Korea to India. India produces over a million engineering graduates every year, yet our rate of start-up companies remains under 10% among students.

For us, the answer lies in the fact that the entrepreneurial habit has instilled itself only within very few pockets in the country. It has nothing to do with the ability of the Indian brain or attitude to life or quality of education. A lot has to do with the prejudice that doing business is

1. Too risky
2. Too difficult
3. Too dependent on luck
4. Too dependent on genius

Rather than look for the real causes why some communities and sections of population flourish in business, we instinctively ascribe it to inborn and intangible qualities. There is a propensity to hide the ladder after the successful climb. A careful study reveals it is not instincts but certain clear habits that lead to business success. We strongly believe that success comes from the cultivation of business habits rather than the so called instincts. This book is intended as a primer in the business habit formation.

The circumstances are rapidly changing recently. More and more youngsters are willing to lose sleep over their dreams. To be one's own boss, to built a company, to launch something different: the spirit of entrepreneurship has arrived convincingly on the campuses.

This book provides with specific examples from our experience, the main thinking and action tools that ensure entrepreneurial excellence. We believe there are certain habits that if acquired through deliberate reflection and care will create a formidable arsenal for the aspiring entrepreneur, no matter what age or position, to find his or her true calling in professional life.

Over the next chapters, we will introduce these habits in their natural order. In the first chapter, we discuss the one habit that must immediately be shunned. The natural loss aversion triggers our excuse habit. We must break it for the other habits to take hold. Most wannabe entrepreneurs stop themselves at the ideation habit. Through chapters two and three, we push the ideation habit into the analysis realm. Then the all important execution habit is detailed. In the next three chapters we reveal the three most important habits in the arsenal of every successful businessman: Resilience, Reflection and Growth habit that ensures sustained, strong growth for all the ventures. The final chapter discusses the ownership habit, a must have that describes the transition of the student to a successful Entrepreneur.

Throughout the books, we have cited specific examples that we have come across in our interaction over the years with successful, not so successful as well as wannabe entrepreneurs. All these examples are real. In some cases names have been changed to protect identities.

If you are already on the path to business success, the content will help you fine tune some of the habits. You can look at your own progress from a new perspective. If you have been thinking for a while to get going, let this book be the guide that assists you to acquire the right habits for Startup success.

If you have never thought of being an entrepreneur but have been merely curious, we hope to inspire you to give it a shot. Read on.

Chapter 1

The Inexcusable 'Excuse' Habit

William James rightly pointed out that 'Man is a mere bundle of habits.'

There are the good habits and then there are bad habits!

We want to address a truly bad one at the outset. As long as you don't get rid of this common detrimental habit, it is impossible to acquire the other good ones that will lead to entrepreneurial success.

Since this book is aimed at those who are considering starting up a business of their own, but haven't done so yet, we are asking you the excuse question right away.

What is your excuse for not starting up, owning and running your own company yet?

Take a couple of minutes to think about it. Chances are that you have more than one "reason."

In our experience, all these excuses can be categorized broadly as follows.

Lack of Awareness

Over the past decade, while visiting colleges to initiate innovation and entrepreneurship development centers, KCC has noticed the students with eyes lighting up and face brightening. In nine out of ten cases, it is for the first time that they are hearing such a possibility. In the case of schools, it is almost ten out of ten. When it comes to starting up business ventures, students seldom get the message from the usual sources. Even when they are aware of the possibility, they are left clueless about how to proceed.

"We have this great idea. What do we do now, Sir?" is the most common question we have faced in our students' orientation sessions.

It was not until the early 2000s, with the IT revolution, that an entrepreneurship culture found roots in India. Ours is a vast nation with an immense, youthful population. So it does take time for new information to become ingrained. When we visit schools and colleges, even the highly reputed ones, it is clear that even after a decade, there is far from adequate availability of good information about the incredible possibilities of entrepreneurship. There are many reasons for this.

Firstly, though India has the youngest population in the world, we are culture that exudes strong respect for elders and traditions. Decision making about career choices of youngsters still rests predominantly with the parents and teachers of the country. And they have exhibited an understandable inertia against accepting a start up culture.

Since faculty in colleges remains the primary source of inspiration and information even in the internet age, their lack of enthusiasm and awareness about starting up gets passed on to the students.

Secondly, the government agencies responsible for spreading the word have been working...well, like how government machinery usually works. This is partly because those who run the show in those departments are themselves not entrepreneurs. Then there is also a limit to how much can be achieved by grand infrequent events that are aimed mostly at political mileage than delivering information. And the Indian population does have a legacy 'trust issue' with its own government!

But the good news is that the national government has now prioritised inculcating a Startup culture in the nation through its Startup India and Make in India campaigns. The trickling effect of these programs will sooner or later be felt at all levels of the society.

Lack of awareness about the funding opportunities and available support for entrepreneurship remains one of the main excuses that people don't start up. Start Up evangelists who can alter the situation are still missing largely from the scene in India. Some exemplary ones are out there for sure. But we nowhere have near enough the numbers of passionate souls who can ensure that all the valuable information is available to everyone who is keen.

We are hoping to do our humble bit through this book as well. Till the teachers and the trusted elderly advisors get comfortable with the information and begin to pass it on, we are afraid that mere ignorance will keep plenty away from starting up on their own.

But not you! At least, not anymore! The fact that you are reading this book means that you have taken a proactive step against the lack of awareness, had that been your excuse so far. Once you are done with the book, you will certainly be aware of not only the possibilities but also the right approach required to succeed in this exciting field of innovation.

There are plenty of online and offline resources available for anyone setting out to establish their own business. It is only laziness that stands between you and them!

Laziness

Good old laziness prevents initiative and following through. Even if all the information is available, all the incredible possibilities are laid bare, ideas flourish in your mind and funding is brought to you in a platter, plain laziness that can block the way forward.

In early 2009, a team of student engineers awaiting graduation had approached KCC. With long uncombed hair falling over his face and a carefree attitude that fit, Mithun had led the group. After the initial discussions in which they shared an impressive idea, KCC promised them all possible help. The boys then simply disappeared. After two months, they showed up in the Technopark Technology Business Incubator (TBI) with a single page typed up. It was, if anything, a step backward from the initial discussion.

Yet, KCC urged them to quickly go ahead with the registration of the company. He asked them to prepare the business plan. After vigorously nodding their heads in his presence, the boys once again vanished.

KCC went out of his way to contact them. Three more months elapsed before a shoddy excuse of a business plan showed up in KCC's inbox. Despite a powerful idea whose potential they fully understood, it was difficult for the team to put in the work needed to push ahead.

Starting Up demands a strong will to act. It calls for 'doing', not mere thinking and talking.

Starting Up takes a firm commitment to executing a series of actions at the highest possible level of quality. The often heard excuses of the lack of 'time' or 'resources' are usually nothing but the glorified rationalizations of laziness. From procrastination to the habit of 'missed call,' laziness manifests itself in several ways in our day to day lives.

Entrepreneurship and Innovation demand thinking out of the box and getting out of our comfort zone, both of which are impossible if we are lazy. It is a round the clock responsibility which takes sincere, serious effort.

It is not in the scope of this book to discuss techniques to get rid of laziness. There are numerous good books available that can help you if laziness is your problem. Even so, the fact that you have read so far, means there is plenty of hope for you.

Comfort Zone

Parameswaran Pillai lived and worked in Quilon (Kollam) all his life. He has never ventured beyond the boundaries of his district. He insisted that his son and daughter find their jobs and life partners also within the confines of Quilon. He had been comfortable with the rigid framework of a government job with its assured salary and pension. He could never understand why anyone would wish for anything other than a government job in life.

With such an overbearing, 'territorial' father figure, it is little wonder that the rebellious nature of the kids soon dampened and diluted into their own love for the same limited comfort zone. Both his son and daughter struggled through several tests, interviews and rounds of recommendations to get their own desks of routine work and assured age-based promotions in the state government's departments. And this was after four years of good quality professional education!

Comfort zone can be geographical, cultural, economic, educational or technical.

It is surely uncomfortable to think about losing a steady income. How would we then take care of the family?

It is certainly uncomfortable to think about the skills that a new venture will demand. Can we learn those new things? Why bother now, school was over years ago?! How about dealing with all kinds of customers from all over the world? Can we put up with their culture much less work closely?

Even for a highly enterprising, resourceful person, unknowingly a comfort zone can develop in the tools they use or the team they work in. It is only when stepping out of the zone is needed, that many realize they had become so comfortable with the status quo in the first place.

An entrepreneur relishes the field of challenges. The opportunities that present themselves as crises and challenges create the comfort zone in which the entrepreneur thrives. So cultivate the habit of catching yourself while slipping into routines. If you start feeling good about accomplishing the same level with less and less effort, you are building up a comfort zone. It should always be about accomplishing better quality and the next level. Your comfort zone should be being at the edge all the time, pushing harder and bigger.

Culture

Culture is a concept that follows right out of the comfort zone. Culture could be look at as the comfort zone that has existed for several generations. In India, a clear majority of the businesses are started, owned and operated by a select few communities. Similarly there are communities that stay safely away from never venturing into the business world.

Different groups assign different amount of risk to the same action.

It is not just in Bollywood or in politics that dynasties exist. If we look carefully, it is easy to see that doctors, engineers, accountants, bankers, administrators and businessmen all tend to nudge their next generation strongly into the same line of work.

The familiar offers a certain sense of safety.

A fairly successful accountant will naturally wish the same professional safety blanket for his son or daughter. Why try a new line of career when a head start is available? There is precious little that is done to discover the inclinations or talent for the younger generation. The intangible assumptions of safety and security skew the argument and cloud the logic.

Yet, to be an entrepreneur means to be exceptional. It is imperative that all cultural baggage if any must be shunned for someone to start up. Innovators are path breakers. They are the ones breaking from the herd. So for anyone with deep passion for entrepreneurship, the culture excuse will never stand.

Risk Aversion

Loss aversion has now become a well researched concept in behavioral economics. The brilliant work by Nobel Laureate Daniel Kahnemann and his fellow researcher Amor Tversky showed us that human beings assign an irrationally large value against loss of something already owned compared to gaining something new.

We are scared of losing our jobs, incomes, relationships, lifestyles and culture even if they are standing in the way of our achieving more. It is a universal phenomenon. The loss aversion or risk aversion is at the root of all the rationalizations we create against venturing into something new.

Even the best of public speakers know the dry feeling in the throat before they commence speaking to a new crowd. It is the instinctive flight or fight mechanism deeply ingrained in the human brain that triggers such a reaction. There is an evolutionary advantage in the fear of the unknown.

Similarly risk aversion is a relic that our brains carry from our dangerous, uncertain lives in the African savannah and the jungles through which our species migrated tens of thousands of years ago. A city may be an urban jungle but the risks in the business world are not akin to being pounced upon by a tiger.

There are of course real risks involved in starting up. But these can be logically understood, scientifically assessed and to a certain extend financially quantified. It certainly is not the same league of dangers that demand a quick pulse and adrenalin rush. Understanding this fact will help us avoid the pitfall of excuses.

At the beginning of the chapter, we asked what your set of 'reasons' were for not starting up. Now we are in a position to recast those so called reasons are simply excuses.

Excuses that pull us back from achieving our full potential;

Excuses that are standing in the way of our living the life of our dreams;

Excuses that prevent us from attaining personal and professional success.

You must break the excuse habit. As you swiftly nip the excuse habit at the bud, the next time it rears its ugly head, focus on cultivating the empowering habits you will learn from the next chapters.

Chapter 2

The Ideation Habit

"A back up battery is what they need!"

"Sell it in larger packets!"

"Offer a customized version!"

Sanjay Shukla, noticeably tall and skinny in his mid twenties, has comments for all the product advertisements on TV. Slouching in the tea brown couch of his bedroom, evening after evening flipping through the TV channels, he has hundreds and hundreds of ideas that pop up in his brain repeatedly. But they last only as long as the advertisement break. When regular programming resumes, these ideas escape into some dark deep secret cave of his mind where they await the next ad break to emerge.

****

"You have an unending supply of storylines, don't you?!"

Vipin Vardarajan thought for a moment, studiously wiping his spectacles clean, as was his habit while processing some serious thought. His friend made that comment the other day at the café.

It was true. Vipin had been at the affordable but borderline exclusive café at least 4 evenings every week for the last year or so. Copious amounts of coffee were downed while discussing story lines for potential screenplays. While his friends have been impressed by his seemingly limitless supply, they were equally worried that none of these ever made to paper much less the screen. Vipin, 28, accountant in a private bank.

****

For the last 18 months, Rakesh Kumar, 35, had been consumed with the deep desire to start up on his own. As the systems designer in a reputed firm in the city, he is occupied most of the day with routine tasks. Evenings he spends trawling the net, reading inspirational tales of entrepreneurial success, watching motivational videos. He has had some ideas. In fact, he routinely has them. He would confess that he gets enthusiastic about some fresh idea once a week, but then very soon his fiercely analytical mind shoots big gaping holes in his thought balloons. Dejection sets in as he realizes the seeming impossibilities and practical difficulties in one idea after another.

To explain better the ideation habit in the rest of this chapter, we will cite the example of these three individuals: Sanjay, Vipin and Rakesh.

We may not be lonesome barons of ephemeral ideas like Sanjay or idea cannon social butterflies like Vipin or self-torturing non starters like Rakesh, but we might know many like them. May be we are a bit like each of them suffering from our own skewed and malignant ideation process.

Branson's Notebook

Richard Branson, the flamboyant founder of the Virgin group, keeps a small notepad in his pocket always. He never dropped the habit from his student days as the editor of the college newspaper. He is quick to jot down any interesting idea. It might appear trite, it might appear impossible. It might be too local in scope, or it might involve inter galactic travel. It might come from a barman in Barbados at 2 am or a doorman in Paris after lunch or the executive on the next seat in the business class at 36,000 feet above sea level. Branson will write it down.

People tell him their ideas...well, mostly because he is Branson and equally because he is a keen listener. All budding entrepreneurs can emulate the billionaire serial entrepreneur in this habit. Ideas certainly need thinking through to become worthwhile. But to get to that process, we must first treat the idea itself with seriousness and respect; wherever, whenever and however it might come to us.

Meet every idea with an open mind and a warm handshake. It might be a lifelong association. You never know!

Observation & Listening

Where do ideas come from?

To answer that it is best to consult with the most prolific idea generator who ever lived. The man who had supposedly the highest IQ ever: Leonardo da Vinci. Leonardo Da Vinci's notebooks are filled with the mind maps that give us a glimpse of the circuitous routes through which grand ideas came to him. Nature, the life all around him, was more than enough for the master to get inspired. Leonardo spent day after day observing the flights of birds and busied himself during the nights conducting dissections. All the mechanical ideas that he proposed, centuries ahead of their final realization by mankind, were all inspired directly from nature.

From the bridges, to the ornithopter and war machines, it was keen observation of the world around him that inspired the genius.

The bird nest stadium that dazzled the world at the Beijing Olympics and the bumble bee robots that buzz around in formation are two recent examples to show that nature abounds with untapped ideas.

The habit of careful observation is vital. An entrepreneur can successfully innovate only when he has clearly detected a need. Observing the market, observing the developments in technology, observing the changing socio-economic conditions and observing one's own changing attitudes are important skills to acquire and polish.

Volumes have been written about the skill of listening. It is an art as well as a science. From the hundreds of conversations we have every day, in person, over the phone, over mobile messengers and email, there is immense potential for inspiration.

Most often, our listening is obstructed by our inner monologue. We are judging and evaluating instead of trying to understand. Many of us are busy preparing our rejoinders, quips, comments and opinions most of the time as the other party continues to speak. This vastly dilutes the quality of listening. It takes conscious effort to provide undivided attention. Paying attention to the speaker instead of preparing what we can say next is crucial. Ideas get inspired and intuition can strike only from paying such attention. Most of the client meetings in business become disasters because there is only talking and no listening. Nowadays there is even more distraction because of constant interference from mobile phones.

Becoming an active listener who can ask the right questions, extract fruitful information and make the speaker comfortable is a skill that needs to be cultivated and improved for sustained business success.

Inspiration & Imitation

We mentioned Leonardo and Branson in the previous sections. When we posed the question about where ideas come from, instead of looking at studies in psychology, neuroscience or philosophy, we approached Da Vinci. It was a short cut based on inspiration and imitation. To know more about ideas, we thought of learning from the man who had had plenty of them.

Successful idea generators and entrepreneurs around the globe should serve as inspiration for us. We are naturally inclined to begin the learning process by imitation. As we have evolved from apes, aping is what we do best!

The imitation instinct can be tapped to help us establish excellent ideation habit. Read the biographies and autobiographies of successful thought and business leaders. They will give us ideas for ideation! If reading long books is not your cup of tea, there are the documentaries and bio-pics to get help from.

There is a tendency carried over from the Indian education system to make the men and women behind the great innovations of mankind, seem distant. Except for grossly inadequate two line biographies, we are seldom told anything about the inventor or discoverer in the textbook. The focus is on the invention or the discovery instead. Students therefore begin to feel that it takes unnatural genius or particularly gifted life to arrive at worthwhile innovations.

Joseph Priestly lives in textbooks as the discoverer of oxygen. The fact that he also invented soda water and published over 150 works included seminal writings on English grammar are seldom mentioned. Students rarely know the adventurous life of the priest Priestly who had to flee to London and then United States after a mob burnt down his home and church because of his controversial writing. Fleshing out the details of lives can reduce the 'distance' we feel from past innovators.

The "distant" feel many have about grand achievements can be diluted by learning about local geniuses. Every society has time and again produced great visionaries in various fields. The achievements of those 'closer' to us geographically and socially can inspire us more to act.

There is a tendency in general in the society to "worship" heroes. By placing them on a pedestal, we tend to "hide the ladder." The brute hard work, sweat and hours of toil that lie behind success stories are hidden. This prevents youngsters from feeling that they too can achieve great things. Very ordinary beginnings of extraordinary lives can be found only when one goes deeper into the biographies.

Aspiring entrepreneurs must see the long ladder that way step by step climbed by the successful business leaders of today. Realizing the possibilities that lie in sustained, steady hard work will inspire you to take the first step. From the life stories of the path breakers who walked before you, you will gather the courage and conviction to strive towards your goal.

Be Purposeful

As long as Sanjay, we met at the beginning of this chapter, makes no effort to note down his many ideas, none of them will ever make it to the next stage. There is no hard and fast format in which ideas need to be noted. How ideas can be noted is as personal as the idea themselves. Branson's notepad is a simple solution. More techno savvy folks can have voice recorders. Just saying!

The important thing is to note down the ideas and then to have a disciplined systematic way of returning to them for further refinement. We must be purposeful. This refinement doesn't mean detailing the business plan. It simply means establishing the idea clearly for our own sake.

Moderation

Consider Vipin's case. Vipin's problem is not the recurring appearance of ideas. It is the overwhelming profusion of ideas. He has no qualms sharing them because he knows more will keep coming. It has been documented that Leonardo Da Vinci famously never completed any of his contractual assignments. He would leave them unfinished. Da Vinci had the habit of failing to finish.

Vipin fails to get started. The act of noting down ideas itself can cure the profusion problem. Putting the pen to paper or typing out onto the computer can instantly change our attitude towards an idea. Once we get serious about a handful, our attention will be consumed by them, preventing the scattering to more and more new ones.

Rakesh stands at the other end of the spectrum compared to the other two. His problem is neither the short life nor profusion of the idea. His trouble stems from his analysis. Rather, over analysis!

An entrepreneur needs to be a realistic erring on the side of optimism. Analysis, if performed extensively, purely in the thought realm, inside one's own head, will move into familiar pathways. These could be pessimistic pathways as in Rakesh's case. Beyond the initially emotionally motivating sprout of an idea, we are better of letting the ideation continue in more realistic terms on paper. Painting glorious future scenarios in mind's eye is certainly motivational. But then it could also be a slippery slope as it has been in Rakesh's life.

There is also a second habitual problem with Rakesh. It stems from the way his mind classifies ideas. Entrepreneurial success need not await revolutionary earth shattering ideas.

Ideas can be broadly classified into three types and all three have potential for success.

1. Revolutionary Ideas

We are talking E=mc2 and Google here. We are talking the motor car and facebook. These revolutionary ideas come once in a lifetime. They are life altering. While we must always be on the lookout for something of that scale, we must neither try to blow our ideas into this proportion unnecessarily nor be dishearten about not striking on such an idea. Revolutionary ideas historically have never happened in vacuum. They appear revolutionary only to the rest of the world. But for the initiators of those ideas, they were products of total immersion over a long period of time.

2. Substantial leaps

If we carefully study the origin of the revolutionary ideas discussed above, it can be seen that for the individual creators, they were only substantial leaps. What appears revolutionary to the rest of the world is product of the immersion and preparation that few individuals went through in their field of work. Albert Einstein was immersed in a patent office problem about synchronizing clocks that led to the general theory of relativity.

Technological leaps like from CRT monitors to LCD panels come through engineers who have been immersed in these technologies. Instant messengers are a leap from email. Certain amount of familiarity and involvement in the current scenario is necessary to propel such substantial innovation.

3. Marginal Improvements

This is the league in which nine out of ten ideas that eventually become entrepreneurial successes fall into. They are simple changes and improvements to existing products and services. This is Gmail triumphing over hotmail. This is Samsung giving Nokia a run for their money in the mobile phone market. This is what Apple consistently does in everything that it gets into.

Adaptations into different markets also fall into this category.

Consider Flipkart as the Indian Amazon. They may also be the correction of the tiny issue that was preventing the massive success of an existing idea. Sometimes it is all about marketing in a different way. Consider the story of toothpaste. Toothpaste existed much before Claude Hopkins designed the advertisement for Pepsodent in the early 1900s. But nobody in the world brushed regularly. It was the marketing of Pepsodent that made daily brushing first a national American habit and then an international habit.

The marketing campaign has been detailed in Charles Duhigg's wonderful book, "The power of habit." Duhigg points out how every habit has three components: a cue, a routine and a reward.

Hopkins had already been a legend in marketing before Pepsodent success. He had already gotten Americans hooked on Shlitz beer and Palmolive soap.

To get them to brush daily, he poured over several dental science books. Finally he found a good cue. The advertisement urged people to run their tongue over their teeth to see the "film" built up. This was the cue. The "film" was bad news. It led to lackluster smile. Then the clear reward of a better, shinier smile was introduced. Between the cue and the reward, came the daily brushing with Pepsodent.

After the ad hit the newspapers, the company couldn't keep up to the demand for three weeks. The product went internationally short. And thanks to a marketing innovation, the world today has healthier teeth.

Such simple innovations that can swamp the existing markets are all around us. Observe & Listen. You will find them. As you embark on building the successful start up habits, pay attention to how the cues and routines are set so that the habits are acquired. The reward, of course, is a successful business life.

Respect the idea

Sanjay's problem can be looked at as a lack of respect, a kind of carelessness, for his own ideas. Our ideas are perhaps the most valuable of our possessions. Of course, as the business takes shape, we will get into the respect and rights associated with intellectual property. But even at the ideation stage, the creator must not treat her creation lightly. Ideas must be treated seriously for them to gather strength and clarity. There must be a habit of putting them down, giving them space and physical realization on paper.

Ideation Clarity

Clarity is the final key in the ideation habit. When an idea makes its first appearance, it may be crystal clear or it may be vague but with that tingling sense of something big lurking just beneath. If we have a physical place, an online or offline file or a notebook, where it is written down, it becomes easy to add the details as they appear.

As we analyze the idea, more clarity appears. But even when initially writing down, it is better to be as clear as possible, so that revisiting it at a later date, triggers the brain immediately in the right direction.

Chapter 3

Analysis Habit

You have an idea that appeals to you, motivates you and is slowly consuming the very fiber of your being. It is a force that is felt throughout the day. It is invading your sleep. As discussed in the last chapter, you have noted it down with clarity and respect. Now it is time to analyze, to tame this wild and powerful beast of an idea.

Filtering & Feasibility

Back in 2009, When the authors met Vinod at the Rural Innovators' Meet (RIM), the annual gathering of rural technology scientists, academicians, politicians, non-governmental organizations, enthusiasts and entrepreneurs in Kerala, he was in the midst of a wildly enthusiastic demonstration of his new invention to a bunch of curiously amused visitors.

Glancing behind him, we could see a pile of complex looking but distinctly unrefined devices. Vinod is a serial inventor and innovator. In his early forties, he had left a steady, salaried job behind a desk after ten years to channel his savings, time and effort completely to the creation of new rural technologies.

Vinod is supremely passionate about his inventions. He has been spending the last five years going from exhibition to convention to conference, adding to his ever increasing list of prototypes each year. Not one of his products had made it to the market commercially, much less made it big!

Where was this talented, passionate, skilled, scientific and socially committed innovator going wrong?

Visiting the Integrated Rural Technology Center (IRTC) at Mundur in Palakkad district of Kerala, it is easy to see that there is no dearth of ideas in our nation. The center is packed with working models and works in progress for various technologies that can drastically improve the efficiency and comfort of the Indian rural life. However it is only rarely that an idea transforms itself into a ubiquitous lifestyle changer.

Let us call that process in the analysis habit, so prominently missing in brilliant folks like Vinod, as filtering and feasibility.

All of us are gifted with the basic human instinct to improve our lives. Some of us just happen to have more fertile grey matter that churns out brilliant ideas round the clock. To be a successful entrepreneur it is imperative to be able to filter the good ones and focus on them.

There are two basic questions that will create the thought filter for any seemingly bright product or business idea.

1. Is there a market for it?

Quite often when we observe a particular problem from a new angle, a great idea can flash in our mind. It originates as the solution to a particular problem. It might be brilliant. But to be a business success, it must have a market. The following line of questioning helps the analysis.

Is the problem that we solved widely felt? Is there a market for our solution or will it satisfy only a couple of customers of whom one is our own ego?! The market must be big enough to justify the investment of our time and effort to create a product. If commercialization is not viable the idea can be shelved for later. It is easy to be misled by our immediate environment. What we have invented might be very appealing to our small group of friends and family. But does it translate to a wider appeal? Imagine a total stranger who fits your target group. Would she be interested in your product? Would she pay for it?

Sometimes, the customer need not be an individual at all. Will an NGO or the government be interested in your product? A good entrepreneur must cultivate the habit of quickly assessing the marketability of his or her idea.

Vinod with his incredibly innovative rural technologies was clearly not doing this.

2. Can you garner the resources to deliver the idea as a product or service to the market, both quickly and economically?

Thousands of innovations are being brought to the market daily in today's world. Time is not on the side of the entrepreneur most of the time. It is a race against the clock to get to the market. Equally important is that the process of manufacturing in the case of a product or delivery in the case of a service, remains economical.

ROI, the return on investment, or the financial bottom line must be paramount in the entrepreneur's mind at all times. Any business that starts off incurring a huge debt is fundamentally handicapped.

Goal Setting

Opportunities can be identified only in the context of fixed goals. Without having long term and short term goals, it is not possible to identify whether a situation is an opportunity or a threat. Let us say your company has been offered a project worth 20 lakhs but it will consume 6 months of your workforce. If your company had a goal of 20 lakh revenue in 6 months, then this is indeed an opportunity. But if your target for the year was 1.5 crore, then accepting this project is going to handicap you unless you can expand your workforce. Without quantified targets, we cannot correctly classify opportunities and hindrances.

Several businesses limit their success or eventually spiral towards failure simply because they go wrong in setting goals with clarity. At the same time there are enough examples of humble beginnings that have transformed themselves into world beaters simply because the founders had their vision well defined.

One of the earliest companies of the Technopark in Thiruvananthapuram is SunTec Technologies. Founded by Sri Suresh Kumar and Sri Nandakumar (hence the SuN), SunTec stayed for more than 12 years within Technopark campus. Suresh Kumar was the technical advisor to legendary K.P.P. Nambiar who set off the Electronics revolution in Kerala, Who founded Keltron (Kerala State Electronics Development Corporation), Technopark (Electronics Technology Parks Kerala),

IIITMK (Indian Institute of Information Technology Kerala) etc.

Two years after it was established, Nandakumar approached the founder-CEO of Technopark, Mr G Vijayaraghavan and confessed a severe case of the entrepreneurial bug.

Mr Vijayaraghavan asked Nandakumar to build an accounting software for the young Technopark. With inputs from the founder-CFO of Technopark, Dr.KCC Nair, Nandakumar, who is basically an Engineer with an MBA in finance, ardently applied himself to the task with the help of a single employee on rolls.

After successfully making this first product that kept on evolving as the Technopark grew, Nandakumar had the vision to approach BSNL. He immediately went national by taking on a client like BSNL. The BSNL billing software done by SunTec was a huge success. Before Tally and other generic accounting software from TCS and Infosys took off, SunTec carved a niche. From the small scale incubation at Technopark, today SunTec's software handles over 3 billion transactions every day all over the globe. A phenomenal growth owing to the grand vision and scaling goals set by the founders.

Once you have an idea that has been filtered and found feasible, it is important to begin dreaming. And from the dreams, we must create goals that are quantifiable and clear. Only then can we proceed with confidence in our entrepreneurial journey.

Mentors

A mentor is not a teacher. A mentor is not an advisor. We can get people to teach us skills. We can find advisors who can help us with our specific questions and issues. A mentor is someone who helps us find ourselves. They are the influencers who combine the right dose of motivation and realism and inject it into us at the appropriate time.

We might have mentors we get to meet on a daily basis. We might have mentors who altered our life's course in a chance meeting that lasted a few minutes. There might even be mentors who don't even know that we exist. But their words and lives can inspire and influence us through books and speeches.

KCC Nair considers Dr. APJ Abdul Kalam, father of India's missile program and former President, to be a mentor. It was listening to a speech by Dr. Kalam in a crowded conference hall in New Delhi that sparked KCC into making technological incubation his mission.

Dr. A.S. Rao and Mr H.K. Mittal fit the bill of exemplary mentors.

As DSIR head, Dr. Rao was the chief mentor for the Technopreneur Promotion program (TePP) in 2007. At the Avenue Regency hotel in Kochi, Dr. Rao and Mr. Mittal, who is heading the NSTEDB (National Science & Technology Entrepreneurship Development Board), Government of India, conducted a face to face program with innovators, When the TePP Outreach Centre of DSIR under Technopark TBI conducted the first State Innovators' Meet in the State.

They mentored 10 startup companies in one hour. One of the companies there, Innoz Technologies went into breakout mode inspired by that short session. Founded by a graduate of Kasargod LBS College of Engineering, Innoz had been at Technopark TBI for two and half years. After meeting with Rao and Mittal, they moved out from Technopark to their own office in Bangalore, obtained venture capital funding from Mumbai and opened offices in the USA within 6 months. He was back to Kerala as a speaker for the 'Emerging Kerala' Startup event the very next year as an NRI. Some mentors have that magic touch.

There are those of the other category too. We have noticed that disturbingly common trend in academia where the mentor assumes the role of a tester. The Business Plan then becomes a bible and mentor becomes an examiner. It is particularly hopeless if the mentors have no experience of having established and successfully run their own business ventures.

As ace psychologist Dan Gilbert points out in his bestseller, Stumbling on Happiness, it is very important whose experience we are trying to learn from. Just like the opinion on marriage while drastically vary from a couple just ending their honeymoon to someone married for three decades, mentors can deliver wildly different advices based on their own current situation and predisposition.

An entrepreneur needs the right combination of motivation and realism at the different stages of growth. Some mentors might be excellent motivators but they cannot provide the reality check for the entrepreneur. Some might be so grounded that the realism quells all enthusiasm. A good mentor is one who adapts to the situation and demands of the entrepreneur while placing the venture's growth as the sole motive. You might have to meet several mentors before hitting the right wave-length match. With a well matched mentor, the breakout mode for any startup is just round the corner.

Business Plan

Dr. Achuth Sankar S Nair, the director of Dept of Bioinfomatics, Kerala University and Dr. Rajeev the director of Asian School of Business are two fantastic, selfless mentors. Under their guidance 7 MPhil students from the Kerala University Biotech division had come to the Technopark TBi. Their product was an impressive biomedical innovation for clinical testing. Yet the focus was more on research and refinement rather than launching it into the market. There was no business plan to be implemented.

A business plan is not a bible. It is a blueprint of guidance. It should evolve and adapt. It should not be considered immutable. The Business Plan is an absolute must.

But there are cases in which the beauty, length and flowery language of the report became the sole focus of the founders. A plan is a plan. It has value only when it is taken to the execution stage. Any investor or business advisor wants to check mainly two things in a business plan. Does it reflect a deep understanding of the product/service and market? Secondly...turn straight to the appendix for the financial plans....when is the company turning profitable?

A great success story based on impeccable business planning is IBS (a software product company established & headquartered in Technopark, Kerala, India) founded by Sri V.K. Mathews. It is one of the greatest success stories of the Technopark. Mathews had tremendous experience working in the airline industry. He had a clear understanding of the underlying processes and the inefficiencies. So when he set about building air transportation software, success was all but certain. Still, it was the meticulous business plan that assured that the business scaled itself seamlessly year after year with many different products added. Today all major airlines around the world use IBS Software for their cargo management and ground control. A small company in Trivandrum had the plan good enough to control the wings of the world.

The business plan must keep on changing as new employees are added and new technology appears. Too much faith in the business plan will turn the company blind to the latest developments in the field. The plan is not the law, neither is it a rule book.

It is the step by step laying down of the vision. It must be flexible but must be respected.

Prototyping and Soft Launch

While a business plan is an essential technique to get our dreams on paper, it is only in the soft launch of a service or the prototyping of an innovation, that we get a feel of the real issues. The prototyping stage is the first step in the physical realization of the product. This stage actually forms the boundary between analysis and execution. It is the period in which the entrepreneur goes through some tests of perseverance, courage, grit and self motivation. Unforeseen and unforeseeable problems manifest themselves we begin to actually build. At the same time, prototype can also provide us with great insights into areas that we had not previously considered.

It was at the famous VJT hall in Thiruvananthapuram that we met Hari Sasi for the first time. It was the venue of the Rural Innovators Meet conducted by Kerala State Council for Science, Technology & Environment, Government of Kerala). A young man from Vattiyoorkavu, Hari had a handful of innovations to showcase. What attracted KCC most was however the least appealing product in the conventional sense. Hari Sasi had an innovative e-Toilet idea. Since he had been told there is no market for this product, he was not too keen to talk about it. KCC knew that was simply not true. Hari was receiving no help to finish the prototype. He had approached one of the leading construction companies in the city but they were not enthused.

KCC connected Hari Sasi to the Kerala State Women Development Corporation who was looking for a social entrepreneurship product. They rechristened it as she-toilet and the prototype was built in 6 months. The prototype impressed the Rein concerts, a startup company in Technopark, later funded by a celebrity businessman in Kerala, who forwarded it to the Bill and Melinda Gates foundation. She-toilets became a reality for the incubator company and the Innovator as well; it is funded by B&M Gates foundation.

Prototype is not just for the product. It is a good idea for the start up to prototype its marketing, office administration and financial analysis. Having such an experimental approach initially will help us iron out issues that could prove disastrous once the company is up and running full fledged.

Thus the analysis of the idea forces us to ask fundamental questions about the workability of an idea. Once that test is passed, we must prepare the blueprint for the business and begin our search for a good mentor. The analysis stage nears its conclusion as the prototyping begins and the company of your dream begins to acquire a physical reality.

Chapter 4

The Execution Habit

Now that the Business Plan is drafted and the prototyping is done, we can proceed to the execution stage. Till now almost everything was planning. The corridors of the universities and incubators around the world are haunted by the ghosts of companies that never made it beyond the prototype. They died with the plan. They never materialized.

We have also observed many who remind us of the words of Ernst Hemingway to "Never confuse movement with action." Some aspiring entrepreneurs can be seen round the clock engaged in frantic activity but with precious little to show as progress. The steps taken by the entrepreneur should be purposeful and goal driven. Wasting time in waiting, getting caught up in endless meeting or not being able to see through delaying tactics are strict no-no for a start up.

Execution habit provides the real action that can breathe life into a new venture. And it begins with the first step of registration.

Registration and Financing

Registering a new company is as sacred and exciting as naming a baby. Deciding the name for your venture can be both exciting and exhausting. There are many teams that split up because they couldn't agree on a name. A good name is essential for business success. A great name is a must for successful long term brand building.

The process of registering a new company varies from state to state and nation to nation. Basically it demands getting all the paperwork in order. The help of a Company Secretary, chartered accountant, registration consultant etc might be required.

You have to decide whether your company is going to be a sole proprietorship, a partnership, a limited liability partnership (LLP) or a private limited company. In the recent years, this process has been simplified a lot and quickened with many of the steps transferred online. Now the Government of India is planning to introduce mobile applications for registering the startup as well as closing the startup at a mobile click! The Hon'ble Prime Minister of India declared this during the launch of

'Startup India Standup India' programme in New Delhi in January 2016.

The execution habit involves seriously and carefully getting the required paperwork done. The legal and financial aspects of the business must be scrupulously kept clean. As you start up, you must develop the habit of carefully reading all the fine print in legal documents, contracts and taxation guidelines.

You can dedicate much of your creative brain to making the company better only if you have the discipline to take care of all the legal and financial formalities like taxes periodically with perfection. Record keeping must be second nature to the entrepreneur. You had embarked on that from the time we started writing down the ideas.

Of course, you can hire highly efficient secretaries, accountants and auditors, but never forget that it is your company, not theirs!

If you are registering as a private limited company, then a capital of Rs. 1 lakh must be deposited. The financial requirements start right at this stage. There are several ways to fund your startup.

If your idea is a science and technology innovation, then there are government grants. For start ups, both state and central governments provide interest free hassle-free loans. In Kerala, the Kerala Financial Corporation dispenses startup loans under the Kerala State Entrepreneurship Development Mission (KSEDM) project. The details and sources of information about such grants and loans are provided in our appendix. Kerala State Industrial Development Corporation (KSIDC) is also giving different types of short term and long term loans (both interest free and interest bearing) to startups under different schemes.

Department of Science & Technology (DST), Government of India is giving Incubator funding, startup seed funding, 'Incubator corridor' funding etc. to facilitate entrepreneurship. Department of Scientific & Industrial Research (DSIR) is supporting technology Innovations is all sectors except pure software development under its scheme called PRISM (Promoting Innovations in individuals, Startups & MSMEs). This is grant support for prototype development and company creation up to Rupees 72 lakhs. Similarly Department of Micro, Small & Medium Enterprises, Department of Electronics & IT etc. also give grant support to startups under various schemes under the Make in India programme. Similarly TIFAC and FICCI are giving grant support for Technology Commercialisation and Technology Transfer under guidance from Department of Science & Technology, Government of India.

Business Angels are also excellent resource persons to approach at this stage. Extra care must be taken to ensure that all the financial documentation is transparent and proper. Ensure that all the documents deciding the ownership of the company are in legally valid format. The very act of framing such documents will sometimes bring to the surface hidden problems.

Building Your Team

The founding team of Mobme presents quite a picture. Mobme is one of the early successes of the Technopark TBI. The founders, the seven young men are all equally tall and athletic. MobMe traces its roots to the benches of the basketball team of the College of Engineering in Trivandrum.

The first business venture of this basketball team was selling t-shirts. To raise cash for their tournament travels, the group bought t-shirts in bulk for cheap from Tirupur and sold them at a reasonable premium in the college. But then t-shirts have an unexpectedly long life, especially in college campuses. So the group switched to SIM card retail as the mobile fever caught on.

From SIM card to starting up MobMe was a natural step. The group visited Technopark in 2005. They were deeply impressed by the infrastructure and the business environment. They approached TBI and met Dr KCC Nair and Mr R C Dutt, who was the Advisor to Technopark TBI. Under their mentorship, Torque was created.

Each member of that team had the flair to fit into a position in the business venture. Transferring an indomitable spirit from the basket ball court was easy. Sanjay headed the marketing, Vivek Technology and so on. The other members like Sijo, Anil and Sony also fit into one of the CXO positions.

The TBI recommends that the a new venture team has one person each to fit into the CEO, CFO, CTO, CMO and COO positions. Torque developed a Mobile accident and crime reporting app (MCARP) first. They graduated from the TBI rechristened as MObMe.

The transition from an individual entrepreneur to a business venture is fundamentally defined by the team building process. No man is an island and it is more so in the phenomenally connected business world. A great team is imperative for a great business. Individual genius is never a guarantee for business success.

Consider the company in southern Kerala run by a multiple award winning young Scientist. The product he had developed is much sought after by armies across the world. The Indian government has thrown its research establishment to fine tune the product. Despite international recognition, business success is eluding the venture. The cause lies in the chronic mistrust habit of the owner. He is so protective of the intellectual property that it is impossible for anyone to work with him.

It is from egoless leaders like Mr G Vijayaraghavan that incredible ventures like the Technopark can grow. It takes inspiring leadership to attract and keep talent around. The business venture is our dream. We must ensure its success. Skilled people rightly placed that can deliver as a team. Depending on your family and friends to form a team simply because of our familiarity with them is almost always a recipe for disaster.

Intellectual Property

The defense equipment company mentioned in the previous section suffers from being overly protective of its intellectual property. But it is important for a new business to adequately protect its IP in today's world.

Megalux Electronics Controls was the second company in Technopark started operation in early 1990s. They were manufacturers of electronic chokes for tube lights. Megalux people worked in different locations. Their establishment cost was huge. There were too many employees in the 4000 square feet facility which even had a conveyor belt in the manufacturing zone. The trouble was competition. Pampa Electronics in Kochi also manufactured the chokes. Pampa captured the market faster. Megalux spent a lot of time complaining against it's competitor for various issues other than concentrating on their business modeling and marketing. But at no point were they thought of patent protection and finally failed to carry on.

We live in a world chokeful of patent infringement cases and IP violations. Billions of dollars exchange hands in the settlement of these issue. It is important for an entrepreneur to be aware of the latest IP laws. Our dreams must be protected.

Sometimes the IP can become a rallying point for the team itself.

When Artin Dynamics was started in the Incubator by students of Amal Jyothi College of Engineering, Kanjirappally and Model Engineering college, Kochi, they had a fantastic product. The electronics device phantom power eliminator (branded as SPARA, an embedded software) had a great market. It would detect if an electronic device is idling and if it is still drawing power, it would cut off. For companies that have hundreds and thousands of computers running, this could save huge amounts. The team received Department of Scientific and Industrial Research grant in aid. But they never started developing a sense of ownership. So the small disagreements began to be taxing and eventually the team fell out. The team split into two different companies, some members sought jobs in other companies and the IP finally became an individual's own.

There is a disturbing trend in the academia of taking patents just for the sake of resume or CV padding. The principal of Nehru College of Arts & Science in Coimbatore in Tamil Nadu is a close friend of KCC. When KCC was invited for a talk on campus, his start up attitude impressed two of the directors. They requested him to conduct a faculty development program. Nehru college campus has seven colleges including College of Engineering & Aeronautics. The biotechnology department was under the Arts and Science College.

Surprisingly all the women faculty of the department was a minefield of patents. Each of them had a PhD with great products prototyped. The head of department himself had half a dozen patents to his credit!

KCC was furious that such a large trove of intellectual property was going untapped without commercialization. He challenged them to launch products within one year. Next year, he was invited back to the campus. In true Tamil Nadu style a huge cut out of KCC welcomed him to the campus. They had aloe vera oil among the several products launched in one event. The oil was named with Technopark TBI tag as a touching tribute for KCC inspiring the commercialization. Now that's not only a great tribute but also good brand recall marketing!

Marketing and Ecosystem

We create companies to sell products and services. People should know us. The right people who would want our products, recognize the value of our services and give us business. It goes without saying that marketing department needs to have as much muscle as the development department in a new enterprise.

It is also important for the company to have the right environment to flourish. It must be at the right place at the right time. The company called Zesty Beanz Technologies Pvt Ltd was simply brilliant in concept. Yet, Lepeesh Parrat and Sanoj, the innovators, remained in the NIT Calicut incubator (NIT TBI) for one year without getting orders. NIT is a magnificent campus. But it is an academic campus. Naturally, the inclination for everyone including Zesty Beanz founders was to focus on research and development instead of getting their software out into the real world and selling it. After 18 months, they began to realize the problem. Mr Lepeesh met KCC at IIM Ahmadabad during one ISBA (Indian STEPs & Business Incubators Association) Conference and narrated his story. KCC agreed to help. He asked them to enter into a co-incubation agreement with the Technopark TBI and start physical operation inside it. Within 3 months Zesty Beanz took off. In just three years, and even before graduating from the Incubator, they opened offices in UAE (Hamariya Free Zone), Germany (Hannover), Brussels (ICAB Technology Incubator), Turkey and the US.

The Technopark TBI became one of the most successful Incubators in the world because of the ecosystem in which it was situated. People wonders how this Incubator could achieve this much success rate! Of course because of the right business ambience around it, a happening place with more than 300 successful IT, Electronics companies and 50,000 professionals working.

Another fact is that the TBI started different business enabler initiatives such as the Technology Business Incubation group (TBIG) and a common marketing platform. TBIG is an association of the Startups through which they can bid for orders and contracts as a consortium; otherwise they will be out of the race when competing with the big companies. The TBIG appointed a Chief Marketing Officer, who was working for all the startups simultaneously who needed marketing support.

The right business ecosystem is required to thrive. A lonesome tree in a desert might be quite a sight but it is in the dense forests that trees can naturally flourish.

It is important to be associated with an incubator or business accelerator in the initial days even if you run the business out of a home office. There have been several successful home-based or garage based companies in the world. Google, Microsoft, Dell and Apple had their nascent garage days.

Yet we would advice youngsters to have an office space. It need not be plush and luxurious. Just a desk or a room or a Co-work space might do, but having an office space creates a sense of discipline and order which can be useful in the beginning.

Entrepreneurs are naturally helpful people. Seeking out societies or clubs of local entrepreneurs can provide excellent resources to start ups. Social networking is a good way to receive virtual mentoring and incubation.

Managing

Managing a nascent company is the management of the 3Ps: People, Purse and Product

The team should be built right and managed right. It is important to provide the right combination of freedom and structure based on the nature of business.

Toonz Animation which had a very humble beginning at Technopark had their distinct employee culture. They didn't succumb to peer pressure and become another cubicle company. The dress code was informal and the atmosphere replicated as far as possible the National Institute of Design (NID) campus. The employees had all the freedom to roam around and get creative. This had a great effect on quality. Breaking the rules is essential for a creative endeavor.

Companies like QBurst proactively assign bigger responsibilities to new employees. This helps them develop sense of responsibility and loyalty. And learn on the job faster. Trust is the main factor in employee retention. The more responsibilities are entrusted to the team member the more they trust the team.

Many young companies resort to overstaffing as a substitute to confidence. Sometimes incompetent staff is appointed with the assumption that they will never be poached by other companies. Recommendations and meddling in the recruitment from all corners is also possible. Here the entrepreneur has to stand firm. More than the product or the money, it is people that make the company.

Needless to stress that the purse or financial management is absolutely crucial! Many companies end up with a lopsided pay structure right out of the gate. The CEO will be taking 25 or 50 times more salary than the average employee. Such an arrangement cannot be sustained. Salary disparity and luxurious wastage will drive good people and clients away.

Getting caught in such showing off habits will lead to dubious sources of financing soon as the cash flow starts to run dry. The founders must worry about ensuring sustained growth and not the brand of car they drive. There will be several easy ways of making money that will show up. It takes serious strength of purpose and character to steer clear of the short term fake promises.

The product or service for which we created the whole enterprise for also needs continuous managing. The feedback received from the market and the industry must be used to fine tune or revamp. Many companies quickly turn to easy money making aspects like training and subleasing instead of focusing on building a brand out of the product. Training should be left to educational institutions or the company can even spin off its training wing. But the attention given to product and service improvement should not be diluted.

Strong product and reliable service is the route to long term profitability. Once the company is established and running fluently, the entrepreneur can switch back on the innovator mode and get back to improving the product. After all, it is the idea that motivated the business formation in the first place.

Chapter 5

The Resilience Habit

"The greatest glory in living lies not in never falling, but in rising every time we fall."

— Nelson Mandela

A huge percentage of all new ventures across the globe fail. Some studies claim that it is as high as 90%. This is one of the reasons we have called the book the StartUp Habit. It is very rare that people get it right in the first shot. An entrepreneur needs to be resilient. When things don't work out again and again, they need to have the habit to start up again and again without repeating previous mistakes. Such learning from experience is the real learning.

Real Learning

Real learning comes from doing. And then doing some more.

Mr Ansar Shahabudheen is now the founder CEO of flourishing QBurst technologies. Ansar has an amazing history of failures and resilience. Straight out of college he started a company in the Pappanamcode Industrial Estate in Thiruvananthapuram. With only passion and no planning, it failed. But the start up bug was strong in Ansar. So he went about it again. And failed.

Believing third time is a charm, he tried again. It wasn't so charming when his third venture had to wind up in five months.

Family and peer pressure mounted. Ansar took up a course in Mainframe programming thinking the skill will make him attractive in the tech job market. This was the late 90s. ER&DC (originally the R&D Centre of Keltron and later on taken over by Department of Electronics, Government of India), which subsequently became C-DIT, was offering the course. It was the same time that Technopark started a student project facilitation center upon demand from outside to impart cheap and quality facility for Engineering students to take up their final year project work. It had become a horrendous practice among engineering final year students to buy projects off the shelf from the outside market where so many small companies are engaging only in readymade project selling (!) business.

Fortunately they were mostly priced out of range of the middle class kids. Even NeST, one of the biggest firms at Technopark, saw an opportunity in this situation and launched training campuses for such projects branded as Cyber Campus.

The Technopark Student Project Facilitation Centre was looking for a project associate from ER&DC. It was decided to recruit somebody from ER & DC through campus recruitment process. Mr Ansar was a candidate for this post. Immediately after he finished narrating his multiple start up mishap stories in the interview, the then CEO of Technopark, Dr K G Satheesh Kumar hired him. While working as project associate, Ansar met KCC. KCC took him under his wing. Like many entrepreneurs, Ansar was very scared of public speaking. KCC made it a point to take him along on the campus visits and motivational talks he was delivering to young student entrepreneurs. He started assigning Ansar small presentations to make in those sessions to boost his confidence level.

In those days, Dataware Design Labs started with a bang in Technopark. Ansar joined this company as he was more interested in project management. The company soon went out of business. He jumped to Ushus Technologies. Working there, he met Binu Pappan and Prathapan Sethu, colleagues with same start up bug.

With a series of bursts queued up behind them, the friends trio launched QBurst and have never since looked back. And Now QBurst is a multinational company with offices in more than 10 countries; where KCC's younger son Krishna started his career as a software Engineer!

It will be great to have a company that gets everything right in the first shot. Nobody is wishing your first attempts to go horribly wrong. But in the business world, more is learnt from failures than successes. You may not get the contracts you desired, or the funding you preferred. These setbacks can teach you a lot more about approach to the business than if everything was handed to you in a platter by fate.

As our former President Dr APJ Abdul Kalam has pointed out, a great leader is one who can manage failures. How you react to a setback and change will determine the future prospects of success? We are not asking you to expect the worst or to be pessimistic. You must be prepared for all eventualities.

Success in business is not something that happens overnight. This is a long road and every lesson along the way counts. So you must have the habit of embracing failures and converting them to great learning opportunities. Business is not a test in which you pass or fail. It is a lab in which each experiment and experience makes us stronger, smarter and humbler.

Bouncing back

To be able to bounce back quickly and healthily from setbacks is an essential entrepreneurial habit and skill. Creating a new venture is not easy. It is thrilling. Our enthusiasm and passion can get us over most of the issues. But sometimes the difficulties become indeed insurmountable. In such situations, it is the bouncing back habit that comes to our rescue.

Vivek Stanley currently works as Computer Science faculty at the Trinity College of Engineering while being the CTO for the successful startup Itmarkerz that he runs with Binu Thomas. But Itmarkerz wasn't their first company. Here's the story in brief in Vivek's own words:

"I met Binu via Twitter. He gave me a happy birthday wish when I turned 22. I thanked him and a few tweets followed. And then we became friends on Facebook. Binu networks really well! I was thinking about a crazy idea called "Intellectual Property Defender" at that time.

It was a system (kind of machine learning based system) that identified sites that provided pirated contents. The idea was to teach a system, to identify pirated contents. He liked it. We decided to make it. We made a detailed design, software, blocking system, and so on. We thought we will develop the system at BSNL's ALTTC. They had all the infrastructure and resources required. However, when I proposed it to the trainers there, they were kind of negative about it. They gave a big NO!

We didn't give up though, at least until another less rocket science idea struck us during its research. It was a mobile payment gateway which we called finnet. The idea was, when we make purchase online, the payment will be added to our mobile phone bill. Technically, this was not such a big deal, but in India, back then, it was a challenge convincing the system.

We made a prototype. We needed a billing API from Telecom Companies. Back then, none other than Airtel had the APIs in India. (In other parts of the world, carrier billing was already there, but in India, it was still unheard off)

We talked with Airtel. They were ready to give the APIs - provided we paid 60% of whatever transactions that happened through them. Now that was clearly unviable. So, we thought, well, the time has not yet come for Indian customers.

Once again, we reached a seemingly dead end. But then, we didn't want to work under someone. We were getting some small projects. It was kind of freelance work. Thanks to Binu's amazing networking. We officially registered itmarkerz technologies by March 2012. It is primarily a software service company. Things were not easy. In fact, it was really tough. But after two years, we have 20 engineers coding with us."

The Itmarkerz bouncing back story also tells us about the need and power of networking for an entrepreneur. In the previous chapter, we discussed Zesty Beanz being stuck at NIT incubator. Networking is triggered only in the right business environment. Using all the social networks freely available, we can create international network very easily sitting at home.

But to realize the importance of doing that, we possibly have to be in a real world business networked environment. The failure may not always stem from business reasons. Sometimes relationships that built a venture might fail. In that case, we have to redouble our efforts to bounce back both in the personal as well as professional fronts.

Subin K Varkey, was one of the students in Amrita Institute of Technology & Science's very first batch. He got Infosys campus selection along with a group of his classmates. He happened to be roommate with KCC's elder son Arun Chand, who is now working in Ohio, USA. Conversations with KCC during his Bangalore visits inspired Subin. Subin resigned in 6 months from Infosys and came to Trivandrum to start up. He set up a company with his batch mate from Trivandrum. The company with a dozen employees was funded by co founder's dad who was working in the Middle East. After a year, the dad returned. Overnight he took over the company and reduced Subin to employee status.

It was a classic case of unexpected investor take over. Subin was completely broken. All his efforts that went into the startup went unrewarded. He got back home to Thiruvalla; mulled over the disaster for four months.

And bounced right back to Trivandrum to start up LogicManse which currently has around 20 employees.

We must cultivate the habit to view failures not as judgments on our efforts or disasters ordained by fate. As said earlier, the world is not a testing center like schools. We view everything as a test to be passed. We have to form the habit to view experiences as learning experiments. Only with that attitude we can truly, calmly reflect on the successes and failures. That alone can enrich our future. So trust your failures more than your successes and they will prove their worth for us in the long run.

Failure as a Feedback

One of the attitude changes that can help you in troublesome situations is to recast failures as feedback. Think of events as the world offering feedback to your attempts. Suppose your company failed to get a contract. Instead of viewing it as a failure, it can be considered a negative feedback to the bid you had made. This attitude will help us convert the situation into a learning experience.

Negative feedback is usually a case of expectation mismatch. You were unable to meet the expectations of the feedback giver. Now the setback is no longer a judgment on your prowess or character. It is rather a one of a kind situation which can help us improve future preparation.

By considering the setbacks as negative feedback, we can urge ourselves to bounce back. Include the swiftness and vigor with which you bounce back to be a natural follow up to a negative situation. Let's say, your company's product was rejected by a much sought after client. Make it a point to be in the office promptly the very next day with a team meeting to discuss what can be learnt from the experience.

Of course, you should not be wishing away the disappointment or putting up fake brave faces. Confess the disappointment but quickly ask what can be done next. Being in business, you are pursuing a lifelong passion. There will definitely be some bad days. But there will always be a tomorrow and our focus is firmly on the bright future.

Chapter 6

Reflection Habit

"Life can only be understood backwards;
but it must be lived forwards."

— Søren Kierkegaard

An entrepreneur's life is dynamic. The day is packed with exciting adventures. The exhilaration of operation at peak capacity is one of the greatest demands and rewards of being in your own business. Quite often the days will end with tired sleep already invading. Sleepless nights are more the norm. Being involved with the team, the suppliers, the clients, the regulators and the mentors leaves very little alone time. But we insist that the entrepreneur must zealously stick to the reflection habit. A few minutes every day and may be an hour each weekend must be dedicated to silently, patiently analyzing and evaluating the progress.

Perpetual learning

The learning in the business world could not be more different from learning in a classroom. It may be suspected if this is why people who shine in classrooms rarely sparkle in real world business. The business world offers perpetual learning. Every conversation, interaction, documentation and even gesture may teach us volumes about human behavior and intentions. Constant careful attention is necessary. Competition does not come in the form of periodic exams here. Competition is the norm. If not with others, an entrepreneur is constantly engaged in a competition with himself to excel further.

Acquiring new skills is imperative in the rapidly changing technological world that we live in. New modes of communication, new methods of manufacturing, new services and new sourcing enter every market each day. Innovations in the farthest corners of the world can impact the rest in no time. We must keep ourselves prepared and poised to embrace the changes that can empower us.

As the startup begins to find its footing, the team members will find themselves taking on more responsibilities. Their initial positions might undergo radical change. Dr. KCC Nair had a Post Graduate degree in English literature but joined the accounts department of the Kerala State Electronics Development Corporation as his first job. When the Technopark project came along, as a member of the initial five, he was assigned the financial responsibilities. Over the next few years, he had to transform into being the Chief Finance Officer (CFO) while handling a bulk of the customer relations as well. And 16 years later, the brand new responsibility of technology business incubation was taken up by him.

Many avenues are available today for us to improve our skill set. Almost every city has good universities offering courses geared towards executives. There are the Massively Open Online Courses (MOOCs) at our finger tips with the world's most accomplished professors conducting bite-sized video lessons. The startups are advised to go deep into skilling themselves by acquiring the 21st century skills.

In our experience, it is the legal documentation and financial analysis that stumps most young entrepreneurs. You must pay extra attention to these two areas as they are vital for the survival and growth of the business. Most often, youngsters have background in one particular area with brilliant innovative ideas in it. The transition from an innovator to an entrepreneur involves getting the other business skills necessary to navigate the business world. Getting attached to incubators can give us an environment to quickly learn these skills, either in our own way or through attending workshops.

Two of the MobMe team of college day basketball players we met earlier, took entrepreneur certification from the Technopark TBI and went to the USA for higher studies in business management. After a couple of years, the team got back together to create the Start Up Village in Kochi. This time the roles and responsibilities that each took on was drastically different from the MobMe days. Startup Village became the a success icon in technology Incubation in the country in 2 years and now different states in India are competing each other for replicating Startup Villages in their States.

Successful businessman, author and motivational speaker, Subrato Bagchi went through several different roles as his business MindTree expanded globally. His books reveal how he analyzed how best he can serve the evolving company at each stage of growth. These days he has the enviably named position of "Gardener" with the responsibility of nurturing young talent in the company to future management position.

At a more practical level, the entrepreneur must keep himself or herself abreast with the latest rules and laws of the operating environment of the business. This is crucial when geographical expansion is on the cards. Legal wrangles and procedural pitfalls can consume too much of valuable resources from the company. Nobody says reading legalese and pouring over pages of boring documentation is easy. But it is necessary. And the more respectfully and carefully you do it, the easier doing business will become in the long run.

Each contract has the potential to make or break the company. So while depending on trustworthy legal advisors, you must personally go through the documents taking a long, hard look at potential problems. So many dreams have been shattered because of careless handling of documents and wild enthusiasm to put signatures on unread agreements. It is your business and you must safeguard it. Personal time during the day is essential for such patient reading, reflection and analysis.

Self Evaluation

As an entrepreneur, you are the business! There must be no cutting corners, no smoothing the edges or watering down the harshness when it comes to self evaluation by an entrepreneur. It is only the brutal honesty with which you see yourself that can lead to crucial improvements day after day. Even when everyone around is congratulating you on a success and celebrating your progress, there must be a certain detached perspective you must be able to assume to look at the developments.

This perspective should compare your achievements and disappointments constantly with your long term vision, with the big dream that got you into the business. Such an evaluation will help you reset your goals, expand your boundaries and recast your dreams to reflect the constantly evolving you. Doing your own business can be the greatest consciousness expanding experience in a productive, creative and healthy way. Indeed, business success is a mind altering drug!

This time allotted for reflection and self-evaluation can go in parallel with your favorite routine. Nietzsche believed that all the truly great thoughts are conceived while walking. So may be your morning and evening walks can be the reflection time. Or you could be a swimmer or enjoy working out at the gym. May be it is long drives (we insist reflection be done on less busy long straight roads if you are tying it with drives) or listening to your favorite music. May be it is long commutes in bus or train, waiting periods or the minutes you spend preparing food.

It matters what activity you tie your evaluation period to. You must be relaxed and perfectly patient with yourself while reflecting on the progress. Rewind quickly through the events of the day past or the week past. What worked, what did not work, what were the obvious mistakes, what sticks out in the mind... the analysis should be honest! You must identify the points of improvement and commit to their immediate implementation. There will be issues that you might want to consult with the mentor. Make records if need be. Keep a notebook for this too. It is your business. It is your baby. Whatever it takes to improve it, we must do, tirelessly.

We are familiar with two of the oldest technology business incubators on engineering college campuses in Kerala. Both have failed to produce any worthwhile companies. In fact, despite having the cream of students in the state available in the colleges, both failed to create a single company that lasted over two years. A business incubator is a venture. In these colleges, they were started with the best of intentions by enthusiastic faculty and administrators. However, there was no personal stake for the initiators.

As time passed, new teams got involved in the management and everyone knew that it was a temporary duty. There was nothing more than a cursory annual report presentation in terms of evaluation. There were no performance parameters, no personal risk for anyone and hence no performance at all. The lethargic administration of the incubator in turn rubbed off on the companies that started up in them.

Contrast this with the 200+ companies incubated by the Technopark TBI in 8 years with more than 90% success rate, one of the highest in the world. This was possible because the TBI had stringent performance parameters and review meetings. They operated like a business in the business of creating businesses. They aspired to world standards and aimed to be the best incubator in the nation. These aspirations and hard work were duly rewarded with national and international recognition. The dynamic energy of the incubator was perhaps the greatest asset that was passed onto to the new companies being incubated.

KCC fondly remembers how MobMe was a brutally honest team when it came to self criticism. Perhaps it was the sportsman spirit that they learnt in the basketball court that helped them. They were quick to take ownership of the screw ups and missteps. Instead of wasting time on passing around the blame, they sought solutions and improvements and took responsibility as the whole team. A basket missed was quickly converted into added energy to score the next one. They insisted on meeting their mentor KCC very frequently to seek guidance. Most often all they needed was a patient ear to listen to their self critical analysis. "Some of their best ideas for growing and reorienting the business came as a result of such sessions," recalls KCC.

Viktor Franklyn, the author of Man's Search for Meaning, provides a wonderful thought wrap up this section. "The pessimist resembles a man who observes with fear and sadness that his wall calendar, from which he daily tears a sheet, grows thinner with each passing day. On the other hand, the person who attacks the problems of life actively is like a man who removes each successive leaf from his calendar and files it neatly and carefully away with its predecessors, after first having jotted down a few diary notes on the back. He can reflect with pride and joy on all the richness set down in these notes, on all the life he has already lived to the fullest."

Reorienting

"What's the pleasure?' I asked.

> 'Planning, I guess. I don't know. Doing stuff never feels as good as you hope it will feel."

> — John Green, *Paper Towns*

Even in the relatively safe and encouraging environment of a business incubator, doing actual business can drastically alter your world-view created during the business planning stage. We are not talking about the unexpected delays, irritating red tape, unlucky match ups, underperforming teammates, overbearing investors, morbid mentors, jealous bureaucrats and the like. Those are all part of being in business and are to be taken in the stride. What you must really watch out for is the drastic alteration of the market landscape.

If you did all the analysis and execution right, high chance that you have a great company in the making. But then market place has increasingly become like the weather. With disruptive technologies, it has become impossible to accurately predict. Thus in the time between your ideation and actual first day of office doors opening, the market you had in mind might have aged, undergone unrecognizably horrible plastic surgery or plain vanished. The habit of reorienting comes in handy in such a scenario. It is included under the reflection habit because reflection only will lead to the insight to reorient the business.

All urges to reorient are not equal. When you study the market and find out the shifting opportunities, it is rather tempting to take the route to easy money. We know several technology startups which quickly jumped into making training their main source of revenue. Bunch of eager graduates were keen to pay the fees to get trained. The company stopped focusing on refining the product or marketing it.

They quickly devalued themselves into glorified tuition centers conducting classes for younger engineers. Initially the students were attracted because of the prospect of getting a job in the company itself after training. But with no business development in the company that was not going to happen. Without the chance of employment, students dwindled and funds dried up. The reputation of the company is tarnished.

It is a case of putting the cart before the horse. If your company is rapidly expanding with new contracts, new markets and flourishing research and development, then you do need more employees. In such a situation a training center makes sense. In fact, it might be economical to outsource training to some dedicated institution or to spin off your own training wing without letting it become a part of the core business. But you need training only because you need qualified employees. The fees from training should not become the attraction for the company. That is wrong reorienting stemming from short term vision and plain and simple greed for quick money. Unless your startup is an educational institution, you must remind yourself that you are not in the business of training people. Quick money is always quick. It comes quickly. It goes quickly.

A great example of successful reorienting is NeST. The company began as a core technology hardware company involved in networking systems. But the CEO Mr Jehangir had a great nose for new markets. NeSt was soon into systems manufacturing. As need for qualified technicians grew, they opened training school. The training school experience was utilized to set up finishing schools. Then a whole cyber campus was constructed. They diversified into several unexpected area including bottled water.

Kochouseph Chittalappilli is one of the most respected businessmen in Kerala because of his philanthropic streak. V-Guard was purely a voltage stabilizer manufacturer in the 1980s. As the competition in the market increased and the market itself shrunk with built-in technologies, V-Guard reoriented itself into electrical goods manufacturing. The brand name and trust paid off handsomely as they quickly garnered the largest market share. V-Guard continues to expand into subsidiary markets in the grand electrical business.

India's most famous reorienting is perhaps the vegetable oil company, Western India vegetable Products, transforming itself into the software powerhouse WIPRO, retaining only the initials of its original name and the sunflower as a logo tribute to the sunflower oil manufacturing days.

Mentoring

For the reflection habit, we want to reiterate the need for a good mentor. It is possible that the mentor who helped you start up may not work for you now that your business is running. The encouragement and confidence building that a mentor can supply in the first days is absolutely crucial. But as the weeks run by and you get into the nitty gritty of running the business and growing, you need a strong support and a realistic coach. There are of course rare individuals who can switch back and forth between the modes.

Ideally, when you are running a business, you need a mentor who has had experience in business. It does not matter whether they were successful in the business. They will be able to better relate to your problems if they have had experience. No amount of reading and listening and learning can provide the necessary edge and empathy that can come from experience alone. Mentors only want your success. So they don't mind when you move on to new mentors. Old ones will always come in handy when you are ready to start up a new venture.

Seek out a mentor who recognizes the value of your reflection, Someone who can understand your apprehensions and aspirations. They should be able to shine for you light along unexpected paths. They can catch qualities about yourself that you had overlooked. When you present your analysis of a situation to them, they might be able to see it in a totally different light. You don't want mentors who will always agree with you or always disagree with you.

A mentor is not a psychologist. Mentoring sessions are not meant to be psychological analysis. That is detrimental. Ask among the other entrepreneurs in your location for good references. They can suggest mentors who have been very helpful. You may even go out of town, out of the state or out of the country to meet with a great mentor. A single sitting can change your life and reorient your business forever. Put in an effort in finding yourself good mentors. It will be worth more than you can imagine.

Chapter 7

The Growth Habit

If you are not growing, then you are dying.

– Colossians 1:3-12

In nature, everything that is born immediately embarks on a journey of growth. Growth means expansion, addition and replacement. When growth is lost, dying takes over. Naturally, this is also true for businesses. Unless the business is dynamic, there is a morbid lethargy that takes over. When easy routes and routines are sought, the downward spiral begins.

Management is nothing but the invention and implementation of new systems to replace those weakened by existence. Every management system comes with an expiry date. It was clearly the downward trajectory of existing businesses that gave you space to launch your own. When they had stopped actively reinventing and innovating, it was natural for an external innovatory to move in. The growth habit therefore breathes new life into the business day after day. Let us look at the main ingredients of this habit.

Vision

In 1998, the Technopark in Thiruvanathapuram consisted of just three buildings. A fourth one was in progress. It was later christened Nila. Pampa, Periyar and Park Centre buildings were in operation. One early January morning, a short stout gentleman arrived at KCC's office. None of the other founders of the Technopark were on campus that day. So it became KCC's duty to show the visitor, Mr. G.A. Menon from Singapore around. While touring the campus, KCC told Mr. Menon the story of K.P.P Nambiar and the establishment of the Technopark. It was only when KCC walked Mr.Menon back to the parking lot that he saw that Mr. Menon had come in a limo. It was the only limo in Kerala at that time. KCC realized that this was no ordinary visitor.

Impressed with the stories he heard that day and the vision of the leader, Mr.Menon returned a month later with the Chandariya group. The huge family business conglomerate came to the park in two luxury buses. They agreed to invest in two of Menon's start ups in Technopark: UST Global and Toonz Animation.

Both the companies began operation in the Park Center. Today they have their own buildings and campuses, UST Global became the largest employment provider in the state. Years later, Mr.Menon passed away during a flight from the USA to Singapore. But by then his vision had already set the two companies on the glorious path to success. When Mr. Menon had arrived, there was no business ecosystem in Kerala to support technological enterprises of huge scale. He went about creating such an ecosystem. By employing local engineers, he created a successful business model which hundreds of other companies followed in the Technopark.

A grand vision may be inspired by several visions that preceded it. But each is unique and carves a path that didn't exist before.

IBS airline management system we had mentioned earlier is also the story of a success triggered by the vision. To dream about serving the world's airline industry from Thiruvananthapuram was a grand vision indeed. But it was the potency of that vision that triggered the dedication of the whole team. Only from such an overarching vision can good targets be set.

A vision should be grand but simple. Companies tend to write clichéd, nauseatingly long, ponderous, meaningless vision statements. Your vision should captivate not only you, but the whole team. It must even inspire your clients. You should have it ready on your desk to be looked at several times.

Targets

Targets or timely goals evolve from the vision. These goals are different fundamentally from our initial start up goals that helped us get off the ground. These are the milestones to be marked off in our long entrepreneurial journey. They are set after receiving feedback from the market and within the company about what our capabilities are.

The goals can be financial or some other statistics like number of clients or contracts. Setting the goals are important because only then we can spot the opportunities and threats along the way. Goals can be set just by the owner or it can be a team effort. The goals must be achievable but not easy. And though it is set by the team itself, it must be religiously stuck to. If accomplishing it looks possible as time goes by, it will be a good idea to kick it up a notch. Being in business is all about improving one's standards every day. So goals must be reset to bigger and higher quantities.

Goals must be quantities. It is ok to have a target to be in the best in the business in the city or state. But there should be a number associated with the "best," otherwise 'the best' is too vague. We all like to consider ourselves to be the best and doing our best. But business is not a philosophical pursuit. So to be the best, we need to attain the top spot among competition. It means producing and selling more than them.

Unrealistic goal setting however can have the opposite effect. We may look for unethical shortcuts. Remember the culture of the owner, soon becomes the culture of the company. If the owner is going to do underhand dealings and unprofessional acts to take the company to the top, then you must not expect any of the employees to be sincere in their work. Unrealistic goals can also lead to sagging confidence. Achieving goals or getting really close to them can provide much needed boost during the initial period of the company. So goal setting during that time must be even more realistic. Without a goal, we don't know where we are going.

There are several companies that set good targets and then continued the culture of modifying the targets to exponentially increase their productivity. A cursory look at SunTec and V-Guard will reveal the effects of targeted actions.

From humble beginnings there have been educational institutions that have reached university level. The grand vision of providing quality education to maximum students was combined with the yearly goals of expanding classroom sizes and adding higher and higher classes.

There are target goals which aim towards achievement and there are productivity goals that set the base for the output from the daily grind. A highly motivated team can put in more and more hours into the projects and also ramp up the output from each hour spend. As the experience of the team increases, there is a natural rise in productivity. This must be factored in while setting goals. A goal must be just outside what could be achieved under the best of conditions with the best effort throughout the target period.

Expansion & Diversification

It is only a matter of time before a great company transforms itself into a brand. Entrepreneurship is a habit. And the start up habit will lead to the successful entrepreneur establishing several other businesses. The experience from the first venture will serve a lot as more and more companies are under the umbrella of the brand.

We already mentioned NeST venturing from networking solutions all the way to bottled water. The famous Indian brands like Godrej, Reliance and HLL showcase a mind bending diversity of products and service. None of them continue to do only what they started doing.

It is not that the company owners gained expertise in all the different areas they ventured into. It is that they had developed the successful start up habits. Once the habits have to be honed, the details of the business does not matter. Of course, there have been many missteps by entrepreneurs getting into areas they didn't know. In such cases, someone else has to be trusted to run the show. That may not work out as positively as we imagine. But as we continue the habit, the chances of success keep increasing with trustworthy managers coming our way to run specific businesses. Armed with the start up habit, all we really need is the capacity to identify a target market and a necessary innovation in it. Rest of the business building will follow through.

Diversification is also important to reduce the risk. With disruptive technologies, the market that had helped us build wealth may quickly vanish. Also with more capital at our disposal we get the chance to enter new markets which were closed to us in our first start up days.

Diversification directly improves the quality of our business experience. We might be able to apply lessons learnt from one business to drastically improve performance in another. And diversification rejuvenates our start up instincts and keeps them sharp as ever which benefits all the ventures.

Innovation

When you startup, your role is a combination of entrepreneur and innovator. You create a company that makes and sells something innovative. But as the owner of a company, as a successful entrepreneur, innovation takes on a different character. While pursuing the growth habit, the advantages and pitfalls of innovation must be recognized for the company.

With success and growth, your company has already acquired a place in the market. In the marketplace when you bring in an innovation, it always creates a disruption. So each innovation coming from a growing company must be carefully thought out. Of course, the company must innovate. Otherwise it faces certain death from competition.

But how frequently and to what scale it must innovate and how much of the resources to be allocated to the innovation are questions that need very serious study. Innovation is not diversification. Here we are trying to build on an already successful product. We are suggesting an improvement. Whether it is drastic or marginal is to be decided. How such an innovation is to be introduced into the market is an equally important question.

Getting caught up in creating improvement after improvement does not bode well for the company. Of course, the marketplace recognizes that when an iphone 5 comes out that next year there is an IPhone 6 coming out. There is a dependability in such a sequence of innovation and the market is aware of the scale of change to expect. Nobody will buy a product if they know that it will be outdated by another product within a few months from the same company.

Look at flipkart.com. Flipkart keeps on introducing new services at regular interval. None of these are damaging its existing clientele. In fact, each innovation boosts its market share. When you are in the services industry this is possible. But if it is software as a service, that demands new purchase for every small improvement, the company is playing with the trust factor itself. Remember the funny ad about the too much long lasting chewing gum!

Some innovations in the same sector can drastically change the game itself or invent a new market altogether. There has always been a market in India for kitchen utensils, but introducing modular kitchen was a game changer. It not only affected the kitchen utensils market, but also furniture and construction industries.

The innovator must carefully study the impact the change is going to bring. It might be possible that the innovation deserves its own new brand. In that case, it is better to spin off a new company rather than risk the existing name and market.

It is necessary to innovate for survival. But the price the company pays for innovation in terms of resources allocated must be carefully calculated. Detailed planning must be involved in the research and development wing of the company. Compete to survive and innovate to grow must be the mantra of the young company.

Technology Acquisition and Transfer

As the company grows and innovates, it will be necessary to acquire technologies from outside. Sometimes the intellectual property belonging to the company might be traded off. We might have an excellent product or service which can be quickly custom-made to meet the demands in Singapore or Germany. But our company may not have resources to do the marketing on our own in those regions. In such cases, tie-ups and partnerships and technology transfers are quite natural. We should never let our lack of resources dampen the expansion possibilities. But extra care must be taken during the transfer. The legal documentation must be carefully checked to ensure that our interests are protected.

Also instead of committing plenty of resources to improbable results in a particular stream of research and development, it might be advisable to acquire the technology from an existing company. The giant technology firms of the world grow by acquiring smaller companies with superior technology for niche areas while having their own R&D divisions work hard to improve their flagship products.

You must be aware of the market trends as well as technology developments around the world. It will be good to spend a few hours each week to keep yourself up to date. Signing up for news groups and visiting conferences are great ways to get relevant information easily.

Any start up owner must be well aware of the Intellectual Property laws of his country as well as the world. Before entering any market or making strategic tie up decisions, time consuming deliberations are required. Remember Abraham Lincoln, "If you give me six hours to cut a tree, I will spend four to sharpen the axe."

Entrepreneurial Culture

Google is famous for its work culture. The company operates as if it is a collection of start ups. Employee teams compete with each other in submitting innovations and product ideas, which are then selectively funded. Retaining such a dynamic culture is one of the main reasons of Google's unprecedented growth and dominance in the market place.

Quite often entrepreneurs transform themselves into managers too quickly in the company. They become the monitors of routine systems rather than continuously applying their brains to improving the company.

When every employee can be made to feel like an entrepreneur with the ownership level responsibility for their ideas, the whole culture remains lean and active. In the growth stage, you must ensure that such a culture is not lost in the establishment of systems and norms. Such a rigid environment with robotic activities has been lovingly called "Corporate Culture." A brief look into successful corporations of the world will show that none of them have such a common culture.

Systems, procedures and norms are required for the smooth running of the company. But they must not stifle individual creativity. It is the power of an idea that got you into a successful business. It is the power of fresh ideas that will help you grow. So the culture of the company should be one of openness, respect for individuality, creativity and passion. In short, the entire company, no matter how big it gets, should be in spirit a small start up. The values and habits that shaped the success in the first days will keep the company in good stead through its life.

IPO and Exit Strategies

The business is as we said, your baby. And like babies, they do grow up, come of age and will be able to stand on their own. The entrepreneur must always have an eye on the exit strategy. It is an essential part of the business plan. Your first idea might appear to be the greatest you ever had, but believe us, bigger and better ideas will come along with your start up habit. So it is important to let go of your first babies and focus on nurturing the new ones. By letting go, we don't mean you stop caring. It is impossible not to care as an owner. We can transfer most of the ownership responsibilities however. It is an entrepreneur that you want to be and an entrepreneur is at his or her best when seeding and nurturing a new company.

One of the most common exit strategies is to go for an Initial Public Offering. Different countries give different criteria for allowing an IPO. It is not something that can happen in a short time span, so it is not a quick strategy. Before IPO, you would have had enough time to put your signature indelibly all over the business. Even after IPO, the owner can retain controlling stake.

In the technology realm, many start ups hope to be bought off by technology giants for a sensational price of course! This is a fairly good exit strategy that can materialize much faster than an IPO. Once a company is bought off, the entrepreneur might bargain to serve as a manager in the larger firm, but true blood entrepreneurs will already be nourishing new superstar start ups. It is a habit that will stand by us for the rest of our lives once we acquire it.

There are other exit strategies depending on the nature of the company and the market. Whatever it be, exit from a company does not mean exit from the world of startups at all. There is no limit to human innovation and ingenuity. And as long as brilliant minds around the world get passionate about ideas, the indomitable start up spirit will continue and entrepreneurship will flourish!

Chapter 8

The Ownership Habit

The ownership habit has the potential to make or break ventures. Outstanding ideas which gave birth to potentially powerful companies have fizzled out because the ownership habit was ignored or never acquired. Of all the habits we have discussed, this is certainly the most crucial to acquire, the easiest to overlook and demands the maximum attention from the entrepreneur.

As we have stated several times earlier, as the entrepreneur, you are the business. It is a cliché whose import sinks in only too late for several well-meaning, smart and passionate entrepreneurs. The transition to ownership from our earlier roles in life like that of a student or an employee in a company is sometimes difficult to achieve. It takes a conscious effort for many.

An incomplete transition is as good as no transition at all. To be an owner, to feel and behave like an owner of the business is drastically different from any other role we have played in life. In fact, it is not a role. It must become our character and our entire personality. The closest analogies are motherhood and fatherhood. The company is your precious baby. Let us look at three of the transitions that are required of entrepreneurs when they create a new business.

From Student to Owner

Student Start Ups abound in the business world. The rate at which student companies are registering in the campus incubators has been exponential. From the late 90s when technology business incubation in India was initiated at the IITs, now arts, commerce, agriculture and science colleges have incubators or innovation and entrepreneurship development clubs. Even some schools like Vidyodaya and Choice Higher Secondary Schools in Kochi have jumped into the bandwagon.

If you are a student or fresh graduate getting into your own business, please take a while to notice, how much your daily habits must change. It is not just the physical behavior but the thought patterns must also undergo drastic changes.

While in college, you were used to structured input of knowledge. In the business world, information comes at you from everywhere. Sometimes no information comes at all and you need to actively seek out valuable information. This could take cleverness which was not included in any of the courses you took.

The syllabus in your college has been reviewed and fixed. It is taught by qualified teachers who are, let us assume, passionate and professional. Thus there is an inherent trustworthiness about the learning. In the business world, you must not only gather information but also judge the trustworthiness or as American comedian Stephen Colbert puts it "truthiness" of the information made available to you.

As a student you had to face periodic examination. There might have been surprise quizzes or tests in certain classes, but they are, let us face it, not life threatening. Running your own company, every day brings to you new tests. Your patience, your will power, your expertise, your skills, your soft skills, your passion, your world view, everything can be put to test repeatedly and frequently. Only the ownership habit can stand us in good stead in this scenario. Completely taking ownership and responsibility for your company will let you operate at the peak attention level and carefulness that is demanded.

College gives us friends. Business gives us partners and employees. You might have gone into business together as friends, but from the day of registration you are partners. That calls for the seriousness, division of responsibilities and shared accountability that friendship never demands.

College life demanded precious little in terms of decision making from us. We always had our parents, faculty, seniors and peers to help us out with decisions. As a business owner, you must make decisions all the time. And realize that there is no such thing as an easy decision. Being the decision maker is the greatest perk of owning a business. Relish it and treasure it, but never forget it is the ultimate responsibility.

The one advantage that being an entrepreneur has over being a student is that re-exams come in all the time. There is no failure in business. Only learning experiences that prepare you better for tomorrow's decision making.

As a student, you may not have "owned" many things. In India, it is common for many students to receive two wheelers as gifts as they get into college. This vehicle is possibly the most expensive item they would have owned so far. The way the vehicle is cared for and treated by the student owner can provide some insight into their ownership habit.

But this is also slightly misleading since many would obsess with such a material possession at the expense of their academic preparation. Student entrepreneurs need not be superstars in their classroom. They need not be rank holders, but to be successful in any business it takes a respect for learning and expertise at least in one narrow area with related skills to ensure business success. The back bencher might be exceptionally good working on the lathe. He may go on to create one of the world's largest lathe manufacturers.

Jyoti CNC is one such business success story. The inspiring tale of Jyoti's Parakramsinh Jadeja has been detailed in Rashmi Bansal's "Take Me Home." 'Take me home' and other works on the exemplary entrepreneurs (a good set from Ms. Bansal herself) are highly recommended reads for all student entrepreneurs.

The college environment does not give us many role models from the business world. So reading books is one of the best ways to get inspired and learn from examples. If the college has a good incubator, they might bring in successful entrepreneurs to interact with the aspiring students periodically. A simulated business environment in your mind, through reading or conversations, is required to get into the ownership habit.

In college, there is plenty of room for excuses. As an owner, there are no excuses for shirking away from total responsibility for EVERYTHING!

From Employee to Owner

Armed with his BTech degree in Civil Engineering and a one way ticket to Muscat, Dr. Thomas Alexander created Al Adrak in 1986. Today with close to 10,000 employees, Al Adrak is one of the largest engineering construction firms in the Middle East. Dr. Alexander never tires of reminding his employees that he had never been an employee in his life. He has always been an owner, even when Al Adrak just had one single mason as its employee.

There seems to be a certain correlation between business success and previous employee status. We believe the transition from having worked for someone else to working for oneself is rather demanding for many. There are patterns of thoughts and action we acquire at any workplace no matter what position we held, that can become severe roadblocks when running our own show.

It is very different from being the head of some division of a company or perhaps head of a subsidiary company to be the head of your own company. We might have been exceptionally responsible and loyal employees. But being an employee, of the government or even a dictator, simply means we are answerable to someone else. It may be shareholders, it may be the real owners, but our focus tends to be in doing our "job" well. When running your own company, all the jobs are your job! We are not answerable or accountable; we are the success or the stumble of the business. You are not responsible for reporting or meeting targets. You are setting the target and you must keep moving the target with constant reflection and revaluation of all the business conditions.

We have seen entrepreneurs with a long employment history get caught up in behavior patterns that they have carried over from their days of successful employment. They tend to obsess about certain details, norms and standards of performance that could hinder the company's overall progress. The owner can have only an ever improving highest quality of performance.

There is an inherent dissatisfaction or discontent that becomes the itch to become an entrepreneur. You might have been dissatisfied with the lack of a product or a service in the market. You might have been dissatisfied with what your job had to offer. It might have been intolerable for you to have another boss. This spark of discontent is the greatest strength of the entrepreneur. If you quell this spark as soon as you become the boss, there will be no growth prospect for the business. The eternal dissatisfaction of the entrepreneur must be closely guarded. The ownership habit which insists on total responsibility and global involvement into every aspect of the business can keep it aflame.

From Owner to Owner

This book is themed on our conviction that there is no escape for an entrepreneur from becoming a serial entrepreneur. You cannot stop at one failure or at one success. You will create more and more businesses over the years. It is going to be a habit.

So when you create a new business, how does the ownership habit affect you? Ownership habit is something that permeates everything in your life. While being a student or being an employee in a company, how much ownership you felt about your work and life, is an indicator of what kind of business owner you will become.

If you have already been a successful business owner, you already have a hang of it. You know that nothing can be ignored or neglected. Complete attention must be paid to hiring, legal, financial, material and reputational needs of the company. You must be simultaneously watching out for dangerous trends as well as wonderful opportunities. It takes the total dedication of an owner to clearly see the difference between opportunities and threats for one may come clothed as the other, a lot many times.

When you transition from being an owner of a business to being the owner of another business, make it a point to go back to the drawing board. Your experience in one business is definitely going to help in the new one, but it is mostly the subconscious instincts that were sharpened with experience that will help. The new business will have new demands, new market place. The old tools may not work. The old you will work. The old you is a better you. But this new nail may not require your old hammer. Approach the new business with the fresh eyes; humility, eagerness and respect with which you had approach every single one of your previous start ups. You must have certainly gotten better at startup, but each start up is a new baby. It has its own needs and character.

Ownership habit channelizes itself through our stern commitment in three main spheres which are discussed next.

Commitment to Self

The owner entrepreneur must be committed to personal, physical and mental growth. You must maintain yourself in good health. Sick days are for employees. The owner can rarely afford it. The demands of a startup can put a lot of strain on the body. So ensure that you have a healthy diet, adequate amount of sleep and definitely exercise.

There is no use building a top company in two years, if at the end of it you are stuck with a medical regimen involving dozens of pills every day. Let the demands of the business themselves becomes your energy sources. There are numerous studies which show clearly how bad physical condition leads to inattention and stupid decision making. The owner cannot afford that. Your health is the health of the company. And that old adage of a healthy mind being a healthy body is 100% true. Let your long term business goals become the motivator for staying in shape and constantly expanding your mind.

An entrepreneur is a quantified risk taker. To make decisions under uncertainty is a difficult job. It is possible only with a certain amount of humility; a deep respect for the randomness of the universe and the fickleness of Lady Luck. These characteristics must be habitual for the owner.

KCC remembers a company created in Technopark by a team of retired government employees. As government employees in top positions, they were certainly decision makers. But with assured salaries, pensions and perks, the fall out of wrong decisions were never taxing for them. They could always draft bombastically complicated explanations and reports about why things went wrong. This had unfortunately become a habit when they retired and created their own business.

Make no mistake; these were highly skilled, highly experienced, very smart individuals in their field. However, they had only sought the glamour of being business owners without seeing the thrill of deep involvement.

The company initially hired an unnecessary 120 people. Well, to feel like real bosses, they wanted more and more people around. Next was a totally uncalled for office space of 4000 square feet prime property within the Technopark. Luxurious offices were created for the founders. Essentially, all the things that should be done only after two or three years of becoming steady in the market with assured revenues were done at the outset with the capital investment. Not to drag the story much, the company wound up its operations in 2 years. It had a legacy of very long elaborate reports and plans to show...each with brilliant explanations about how everything went wrong. Everyone felt like a boss, not one felt like an owner!

The owner cannot let greed or fear overpower him. This means building up a steely character. Of course, we are in business for profit. But there is a big difference between building up a strong company with steady profit and wanting quick richness. On the other hand, if the owner is too timid to take risks and seek out opportunities, there will be no growth. The delicate balance between expansion and consolidation comes from feeling a deep sense of ownership and commitment to oneself. The owner will be prepared to say "No" a lot more times to temptations.

Commitment to the family

By family, we mean the people directly dependent on you and also those who worry about you sincerely. Starting and running your business will consume almost all your time. It is your family who will miss your presence the most. You might miss out on several family events, celebrations. You will get very little quality time to spend with your loved ones. You may not be able to give them the attention they deserve. This fact must be recognized and planned for. Because if our family life and our close relationships are strained, it will immediately affect our performance as entrepreneurs. We are not islands of fragmented consciousness. It is impossible to switch off the family mode and switch on business mode as soon as we arrive at workplace.

The family must be made to recognize the implications of your business ownership. After all, it is mostly our family which will benefit from the business success. If you are getting into business or use your workplace as an excuse to get away from the family, then it is a wrong motivation which will never bring success. You must beg for the patience of the family as you get the business off the ground. Make a firm commitment to keep increasing the time and effort you spent for the family over the course of time as certain business systems begin to work smoothly. When you are with family (and friends), turn off the cell phone. Messages can be checked one hour later. Not letting business invade family time will in turn help us make sure that family matters don't invade business hours.

Commitment to family will also help us in decision making by keeping the long term and ethics in perspective. Your business reputation has direct implications for your family. You have no right to ruin the next generation by succumbing to greed or fear. Family, when treated sacredly, can form the fundamental pillar for business success.

When couples go into business together, they are becoming partners of a new kind. Careful discussions and deliberations in the beginning are an absolute must.

You cannot switch the business roles and family roles seamlessly. Accept that there is only the owner's role. But that role demands that you be a very good husband or wife as well. Any tensions must be solved by honest discussions as soon as they arise. This is good business practice as well. Own your life! Own your family! Own your loved ones!

Commitment to the society

Indian political scene is littered with politicians who believe they can be happy or their families can be joyful and secure at the expense of the rest of the society. No business owner should subscribe to this stupid illusion. Only healthy, thriving, moral and progressive societies can feed good businesses.

The ownership habit insists that you are 100% ethical in all the dealings. Any tendency to cut corners or corruption will quickly become a habit because it appears to be so much easier than the proper route. Unfortunately the price to be paid for initial ease will be too high in the end, not to mention the disappearance of peace of mind forever.

You business is not a charity. It is a profit making venture. But it must provide benefits for the society. A successful entrepreneur must try to maximize the employment in the society. If we focus on providing a million jobs instead of making a million dollars, the million dollars will soon follow. It is an ethical way of expanding your business which will provide more tangible benefits than fixing purely financial growth targets. A company is a company of men and women. Aiming for the greater common good will also propel us to make our workplace more friendly and uplifting.

It will not be possible to satisfy all the people all the time, but as Mother Teresa pointed out we can do little things with great love. A successful entrepreneur is inherently a philanthropist. Remember how many charity organizations and foundations have been created by successful industry leaders world over; Governments are making laws to direct the corporate companies to fund and promote CSR (Corporate Social Responsibility) initiatives. Human beings are social creatures. It is not surprising that except for the real psychopaths, most of us are blessed with a compassion that pushes us to improve the lot of those around us. It is an instinct that can be tapped into further energizing our ownership habit.

Own your society! Own your nation! Own the world!

Printed in the United States
By Bookmasters